Is There Something Something George Eastman Would Have Done?

The Decline and Fall of Eastman Kodak Company

Second and Revised Edition

by Paul Snyder

ISBN-10: 1479363669
EAN-13: 9781479363667

Table of Contents [Excluding Point III]

1 - ARGUMENT

Investors, financial analysts, and even the general public assume that Kodak's serious problems began in the digital era. Would that it had been so. Kodak's problems had their origin in corporate mistakes almost fifty years earlier.

The author's experience with photography began in approximately 1955 when his father bought him a Brownie Holiday camera, which used size 127 roll film. The next year his father bought him a Hawkeye camera with a flashgun so that he could take pictures indoors. The author spent many Saturday nights in his cousin's basement processing black and white photos in smelly trays of developer, stop bath, and fixer. Because it was extremely difficult, time-consuming, and expensive to enlarge and print color negatives, the author persuaded his father to buy him a 35mm camera so he could take color slides.

The first 35mm camera owned by the author was a Signet 40. By today's standards it was primitive. It had no light meter. Focusing was done with a crude split-image rangefinder. At that time, two types of color slide film were popular. The original Kodachrome film had a speed of only 10. Ektachrome had a speed of 32. While Kodachrome accurately reproduced skin tones and had a relatively high contrast, Ektachrome had slightly more grain and produced images with a bluish tinge. Ektachrome was popular because it could be processed quickly by private laboratories or at home, while Kodachrome could be processed only by Kodak.

By the time the original Kodachrome was replaced by Kodachrome II with a speed of 25, the author's Signet 40 was replaced by a Kodak Retina Reflex. It was one of the first American single-lens reflex (SLR) 35mm cameras. It was a heavy, bulky metal camera assembled in Germany. It had a built-in light meter and partially interchangeable lenses. Subsequently, the author acquired a Retina Reflex S, which had fully interchangeable lenses. With a 135mm telephoto lens, it was possible to take pictures of soccer games, baseball games, and even wildlife. The author took thousands of color slides with the Retina Reflex S.

Retina cameras were Kodak's traditional top-line 35mm cameras for advanced amateurs. They were manufactured by a Kodak subsidiary in Stuttgart, Germany. All of the Retina cameras were of very high quality. They were highly sought after by advanced amateur photographers. Even today, the folding model Retina IIIC is prized by camera collectors.

In 1969 Kodak ceased production of Retina cameras. The decision to cease production was never fully explained by Kodak management. One can speculate that management feared that an increase in the value of German currency (a decline in the value of the dollar) would make German cameras too expensive for the American market. More likely, the reason for stopping production was a misunderstanding by current executives of George Eastman's methods. Eastman had sought to simplify photography for the general public. Thirty-five millimeter film came in a spool. If the film leader from the spool were not properly pulled forward to engage two sprockets in the northerly and southerly positions on the take-up wheel, the film would not be advanced through the camera and would not be exposed. Kodak waited for almost thirty-seven years after its founder's death until it finally decided that it was too difficult for the general public to load and unload 35 mm cameras.

The decision to abandon the 35mm camera market was one of the biggest mistakes ever made by an American company. Until that time the Japanese had never been serious contenders in the US camera market. The 35mm camera was invented and popularized by the German corporation, Leica. Its small size made it ideal for travel, location, and news photography. Some consider the Leica M3 to be the best 35mm camera ever made. Certain Japanese competitors got their start by copying Leica rangefinder cameras, but it was the 35mm SLR camera that made the Japanese dominant. They had focal plane shutters, fast interchangeable lenses, and electronic speed lights. By installing the focal plane shutter inside the camera itself, the lenses did not need individual shutters and were lighter and easier to carry and use. In Japanese SLRs the film advance lever was on the upper right top, in contrast to the Retina Reflex cameras, where the film advance lever was inconveniently located on the bottom.

Kodak surrendered the entire 35mm camera market to the Japanese. Kodak did so at the precise time when the 35mm camera market was about to explode in popularity. Kodak could not foresee that electronic automation would simplify photography. It was the Japanese who took advantage of microelectronics to popularize the point-and-shoot 35mm camera.

In the early 1970s, shortly after the author bought his first Nikon F, he had lunch with a fellow member of the Rochester Jaycees in the Kodak management cafeteria at 343 State Street. "Why," he asked, "did Kodak abandon the 35mm camera market to the Japanese?" There, sitting almost directly beneath the faded color enlargement of a serious-looking George Eastman, the Jaycee said, "At Kodak we don't worry about the market. We *are* the market."

And that was the essence of the problem. Kodak's success led to corporate hubris, which caused its untimely exit from some markets (35 mm cameras), its untimely entrance into other markets (inkjet printers), and caused it not to enter other markets (cell phone cameras), and to enter the wrong markets (instant cameras, pharmaceuticals).

Kodak had profited from the long transition from black-and-white photography to color. It had made photography an integral part of American life. Its giant color transparencies dominated the main hall in Grand Central Station. Its yellow film boxes were sold worldwide. If anyone in 1980 had suggested that Kodak would file for bankruptcy, he would have been called stupid.

Kodak had always been a growth stock. "You don't sell Kodak." When trusts and estate lawyers gave estate-planning lectures to Rochester attorneys, they spoke of Rochester as the home of "old money."

The famous Kodak Park tour attracted thousands of visitors each year. Tour groups were led inside vast factories and shown enormous machines, conveyor belts, and film assembly lines. The highlight was the visit to the darkrooms, where film was developed under eerie green safelights. Upon reentering daylight, the tourists were often told "We don't employ blind people in darkrooms." In retrospect, they did employ "blind people;" not in a literal sense, but in a managerial sense; not on assembly lines, but on the higher floors of Kodak's office building at 343 State Street. What follows is a "Brandeis Brief" account of that failure of vision by the once pre-eminent imaging company in the world.

Author's suggestion: read Point III first, before reading Points I and II. The documentation therein required 571 footnotes. The analysis and update in Point III ties together into a single argument the enormous amount of facts and numbers in the first two sections.

POINT - I

BEFORE THE FINANCIAL CRISIS

2 - THE DECLINE BEGINS
(1972–1991)

Initially, Kodak's decision to abandon the market for 35mm cameras looked wise. To simplify loading and unloading film, it invented the Instamatic Cartridge. The size 126 cartridge was introduced in 1963. It eliminated the need to thread the film leader into sprockets on the take-up wheel. With motorized film advance, and automatic motorized rewind at the end of each roll, it was an enormous success. Kodak even created an Instamatic version of its SLR Retina—the Instamatic Reflex. By 1972 Eastman Kodak was a glamour stock with earnings growing at a 30 percent rate. It was a full-fledged member of the "Nifty Fifty."

Polaroid was its only serious domestic rival. Other domestic manufacturers were no threat. General Aniline and Film (GAF) produced low-quality cameras under the ANSCO brand name. Their film was grainy and unpredictable. The GAF film speeds were never what the company claimed.

The very name "Instamatic" exemplifies Kodak's fixation with Polaroid Land Cameras. Instamatic cameras did not produce instant photos. Only Polaroid cameras were really instant cameras. Polaroid photographs were pulled outside the camera where they developed in full daylight.

The black-and-white Polaroid process, however, was messy and inconvenient. Each picture had to be quickly smeared with a sticky, foul-smelling coater stick to prevent fading. Polaroid solved the coater problem with the introduction of the SX-70 camera in 1972. It was then no longer necessary to peel apart photos and coat them.

A source—one the author believes to be truthful and reliable—informed him that in the early 1960s Kodak's research scientists were "taking apart" Polaroid cameras. They were obviously seeking to reverse-engineer the Polaroid "picture in a minute" process.

This ill-advised effort to plagiarize another company's technology caused Kodak to lose its competitive focus. It distracted the company from the growing Japanese threat. In fact, Fuji Film introduced 400 speed film before Kodak.

The financial press began to doubt Kodak's decision to compete against Polaroid. The June 20, 1977, issue of *Business Week* had a cover story entitled "Kodak: The Market Manhandles a Blue Chip." The subtitle of the article asked, "Have investors overreacted to the situation at Kodak?" The article described Kodak's strategy of using dealer rebates, suggesting it was trying to build market share by selling below cost.

Kodak's instant cameras were "me-too" products with no competitive advantage over Polaroid products. What could the Kodak instants do that the Polaroid instants could not do? Apparently, Kodak never asked this question.

Before Kodak entered the instant camera market, investors anticipated large profits. When a Kodak annual report had a photo of the future camera, stockbrokers got on the telephone and told their customers, "Now you've got to buy the stock."

They never considered that stock prices go in both directions—down as well as up. At the height of Kodak's arrogance, when the waiting list for membership in the Tennis Club of Rochester was almost five years, it was impossible to conceive of a major decline in the price of Kodak stock.

When Kodak introduced its instant cameras, Polaroid immediately sued for patent infringement. On October 13, 1985, Polaroid announced that it had secured an injunction barring Kodak from selling instant cameras and film after January 9, 1986.[1] Kodak never had the

---

1 As reported in the Oct. 14, 1985, issue of *The Wall Street Journal.*

foresight to realize that the truly instant camera would be electronic—that is, digital, and not chemical-based.

Meanwhile, the unexpected decline in the value of Kodak stock led to worries about a hostile takeover. Wall Street was in the "Greed Is Good" era of Boesky, Milken, and others. To diversify its business away from the increasingly competitive photography business, and to make a takeover more complicated, Kodak purchased Sterling Drug, whose principal product was Bayer aspirin. The only thing in common between the two companies was that they both produced chemicals. It was a complete mismatch. Pharmaceuticals were a highly regulated life-sciences business, requiring three different phases of clinical testing, relying heavily on statistical analysis. Eastman Kodak had no experience in dealing with the Food and Drug Administration (FDA).

Kodak purchased Sterling Drug for $5.1 billion. The purchase was the subject of intense ridicule among investors. A *Business Week* article on this subject featured a photograph of a smiling President Kay R. Whitmore holding an Instamatic Camera, surrounded by oversized boxes of 35mm film.[2] Perhaps Kodak had hoped for a blockbuster drug from Sterling. With no experience in managing a pharmaceutical company, Kodak's purchase was doomed from the beginning. The only beneficiaries of the purchase were the Wall Street arbitrageurs and

---

2 "Kodak May Wish It Never Went to the Drugstore," *Business Week*, Dec. 4, 1989.

stockholders of Sterling, who received money amounting to 35 times Sterling's earnings. Kodak's CEO spent $5.1 billion of the shareholders' money on a losing Lotto ticket. Kodak had transformed itself from a photography company into a conglomerate.

So fond of quoting George Eastman in its glossy annual reports to shareholders, Kodak could have avoided all the myriad problems with its Sterling Drug purchase had the board of directors asked the CEO one or two simple questions: (1) What would George Eastman have done, and (2) specifically, Would George Eastman have purchased Sterling Drug?

Meanwhile, Kodak's traditional photography business was having its own problems. Kodak decided to change the format size of its conventional color negative film to force consumers to buy new products. The strategy could be called progressive obsolescence. The Instamatic camera would be made obsolete by the Disc camera. The film would be the same, but consumers would be forced to upgrade because Instamatic cartridges would not fit the Disc camera. However, the Disc negatives were so small that ordinary prints were too grainy. The prints were shabby-looking and unpopular with consumers. Compared to 35mm prints, the Disc prints were atrocious. So how did Kodak respond? When it lost its patent lawsuit to Polaroid, it gave the owners of Kodak instant cameras three choices: (1) exchanging the Kodak Instant camera for a Kodak Disc camera (which it would later stop making), (2) $50 worth of coupons of other Kodak products, or (3) one share of Kodak stock (selling then for $47.50 which by 2012 would be almost worthless).[3]

At this point one is tempted to stop and ask why almost everything Kodak touched turn to poison. How could one company have such a losing streak? Was it bad luck, or was something else at work?

Perhaps the answer can be found in another unsuccessful Kodak acquisition. In 1981, the company purchased Atex, Inc. for $79.8 million. It made text publishing systems.[4] Within two years, Atex suffered defections by its founders, and its technology was becoming obsolete.[5] The problem was that Kodak's massive bureaucracy failed to respond in a timely manner to the needs of the marketplace. It mistakenly assumed it could impose its will on the market, at its own slow-as-molasses pace. By 1987 Kodak had named its third management team at Atex.

In 1986, Kodak began its first in a long series of restructurings. Just as the Roman legions were withdrawn from the provinces, it progressively cut its work force, leaving

---

3 For more information see "Coping with 16.5 Million Headaches," at page 38 of the Mar. 3, 1986, issue of *Fortune*.

4 See "Kodak Facing Big Challenges in Bid to Change," *The Wall Street Journal*, May 22, 1985, 6.

5 See "Embattled Kodak Enters the Electronic Age,", *Fortune*, Aug. 22, 1983, 120

few employees by the time of its bankruptcy in 2012. In 1985, Kodak employed 128, 950 people. Its first restructuring planned to cut 10 percent—almost 13,000 people.[6]

By 1988, the population of Rochester began to show increasing hostility to Kodak. Twenty-three toxic chemicals were allegedly seeping into the groundwater near residences neighboring Kodak Park.[7] In 1989, the hostility would become widespread public anger. The residents of Rochester would realize that executive compensation at their biggest corporate employer was not based on corporate performance.

It was highly unusual in the "don't make waves" conservative nonconfrontational climate of Rochester for six letters to the editor on the same day to voice public criticism of corporate compensation and corporate performance. But this is exactly what happened in the "Speaking Out" page of the Rochester *Democrat and Chronicle* on September 5, 1989. The first letter demanded that CEO Chandler should quit. The second letter adversely compared the then present quality of Kodak's senior management to Kodak's former leaders. The third letter argued that CEO Chandler was a failure. The fourth letter argued for freezing the salaries of Kodak's top management. The fifth letter worried about the size of Polaroid's award of damages. The sixth letter did not mention Kodak, but

---

6 *The Wall Street Journal,*" Feb. 12, 1986, 2.

7 See "Not a Pretty Picture: The Toxic Spills at Kodak Park," *Business Week*, Sept. 12, 1988, 39.

criticized the gap between the compensation of ordinary workers and company executives.

One would think that if a publicly traded company earned less money than the year before, that its managers should be paid less. After all, capitalism is not merely about rewards. While achievement should be rewarded, failure should be penalized. Yet, on September 10, 1989, the Rochester *Democrat and Chronicle* reported that Chairman Chandler's annual pay increased 20 percent, and that President Whitmore's annual pay increased 24 percent.

Despite the decline in corporate earnings, despite layoffs, despite restructurings, despite the loss of the lawsuit to Polaroid, and despite failed acquisitions, senior management's pay went up. Bad results were rewarded. Was this rational? If company profits declined, why should senior management's pay increase? Did management treat the company as a personal piggy bank? Was it fair to lay off workers and increase executive salaries? Did the executives ever consider how this would lower company morale?

Shortly thereafter, the September 19, 1988, The *Wall Street Journal* had a front page story entitled "*Last Chance*: Kodak Chief Is Trying, for the Fourth Time, to Trim Firm's Costs." It referenced the resignation demands in the Letters to the Editor in Rochester's daily newspaper.

Day after day, month after month, year after year, Kodak continued to underestimate electronic imaging. In 1990, Kodak's internal forecast was that in twenty years, by 2010, 30 percent of all photographs would be through electronic imaging.[8] Conversely, the company believed that in 2010, 70 percent of all photographs would be through traditional film and chemicals. It was too painful for Kodak to face the reality that electronics would make film obsolete. For the next two decades, Kodak operated under the incorrect assumption that film would continue to be more popular than electronic cameras. Kodak failed to learn from the lesson of mechanical calculators being replaced by electronic ones. All the signs were there for them to see. It was a self-inflicted corporate blindness. Rather than adopt the new electronic technology, it stubbornly tried to prolong the life of film-based photography. This mind-set was responsible for the Photo CD.

The Photo CD was a half-hearted foray into electronic imaging. When a roll of photographic film was developed, the consumer would have the option of paying an extra $20 for a Photo CD, which contained one hundred electronic images.[9] It was an intermediate step between film and filmless photography. But why would a consumer pay an extra $20 for film to create an electronic image if

---

8 *The Wall Street Journal*, July 16, 1990.

9 See "The New Look of Photography," *Fortune*, July 1, 1991, 40.

this could be done directly by using an electronic camera without film?

Kodak tried to accelerate decision-making not only by reducing the head count, but also by establishing small business units with exotic names to build innovative products outside its bureaucracy. It hoped to emulate IBM's experience in developing the PC. It created fourteen separate small companies but did not give the managers equity stakes in the companies.[10] All of the companies were sold or closed down.

By the beginning of the 1990s Kodak was a troubled company. In October of that year, a federal judge awarded Polaroid $909.5 million in damages. Kodak's Disc camera was stopped in 1988. Since 1983 it had let go 25,000 employees.[11] Then in 1993, several top executives and software engineers resigned from Kodak's Photo CD unit, frustrated with Kodak's bureaucracy.[12] The crisis was soon to worsen.

---

10 *The Wall Street Journal,* Aug. 17, 1990, B1.

11 *"Forbes,"* Nov. 26, 1990, 67.

12 *The Wall Street Journal,* June 4, 1993.

3 - CEO CHANGE
(1991–1993)

Kodak's first restructuring in the 1990s was seen as a positive development. The large headline in the August 13, 1991, Rochester *Democrat and Chronicle* stated, "3,000 Kodak jobs will be eliminated." The company offered early retirement benefits without any penalties. It offered full retirement benefits to employees (1) whose total age and years of employment was at least seventy-five, and (2) employees at least fifty-five years old, who worked for Kodak at least ten years. As a further gesture of generosity, Kodak offered monthly payments to retiring employees until they were eligible for early payment of Social Security at age sixty-two. Page 7A of the newspaper profiled one employee who called the package "Christmas money." In another article on the same page entitled "Local Leaders See Long-run Gain," the newspaper wrote, "And best of all, the move should help the company remain competitive for years to come."

After this brief interlude of allegedly good news, the bad news resumed. Haloid Corporation had used a dry electrophotographic process invented by Chester

Carlson to produce the Xerox 914 copier. A once obscure Rochester competitor, it eventually dominated the office equipment market for copying machines. It changed its name to Xerox Corporation, and made Kodak's wet photocopying system, Verifax, obsolete. As Xerox's patents expired, Kodak entered the dry photocopier business. In the third quarter of 1991, the Kodak office products business lost $20 million. On November 8, 1991, Kodak announced that several top executives of that division were leaving.[13]

In December 1991, Kodak learned that twice as many eligible employees sought early retirement: 6000 people.[14] While its Eastman Chemical division continued to prosper, the rest of Kodak was severely troubled. It was estimated that Kodak paid about $350 million in annual interest on the debt it incurred to acquire Sterling Drug, but that in 1991 Sterling Drug had earned a profit of only $379 million. No blockbuster drug had emerged since the Kodak acquisition. Also, its prior restructurings did not produce the $200 million in annual after-tax savings it had anticipated.[15]

By January 1993, it was obvious that Kodak's strategy was not working well enough. The local newspaper warned that Kodak might cut 3,000 more workers,

---

13 See Nov. 8, 1991 *Wall Street Journal*, A4.

14 Rochester *Democrat and Chronic*, Dec. 4, 1991, 8D.

15 See April 8, 1992 *The Wall Street Journal*, B4.

including scientists from its research laboratories. It published a graph on its front page showing how Kodak's Rochester workforce declined from 60,406 in 1982 to 39,600 in 1991.[16] "We Are All Positive and Have Faith" was the headline in the local newspaper after Kodak decided to cut 2,000 employees. "This will be the year that many of the plans will reach fruition," CEO Whitmore was quoted as saying.[17]

Even Kodak's core profit engine of amateur photographic film came under attack. Lower-priced generic versions of color negative film began to compete with Kodak's higher priced products. Kodak's foray into the prescription drug business should have alerted it to the dangers of generic competition. Generics were a growing threat to brand-name drugs. Why pay more for a brand-name drug if a chemical equivalent were available at a lower price? Why pay more for a roll of film if a private-label generic were available at a lower price? Why overpay for essentially the same product?

In 1992, Kodak's board of directors reduced CEO Whitmore's bonus by 70 percent.[18]It was the Steffen controversy in 1993 that caused his downfall.

On January 11, 1993, Christopher J. Steffen was appointed Chief Financial Officer (CFO). He was seen by

16 See Rochester *Democrat and Chronicle*, Jan. 8, 1993, front page.

17 Rochester *Democrat and Chronicle*, Jan. 20, 1993.

18 *Business Week*, February 1, 1993, 25.

Wall Street as a catalyst for improving corporate performance at Kodak. He had previously helped turn around two other industrial companies, Chrysler and Honeywell. Within three weeks of his appointment, Kodak stock had increased 17 percent or about $2 billion.[19] By April 28, 1993, Kodak stock had increased by about $3.45 billion in value.[20]

April 28, 1993, began with a front page article in *The Wall Street Journal* calling attention to the different management styles of the CEO and CFO. The article was entitled: " Contrasting Images: The New Finance Chief at Kodak Has a Style Quite Unlike His Boss's—While Chairman Whitmore Abhors Cutting Workers, Steffen Doesn't Flinch—Profits Aren't a Pretty Picture." It compared the glacially slow pace of Whitmore to the more dynamic Steffen. The last paragraph hinted that Steffen would be elected to the board of directors at the upcoming annual meeting on May 12, 1993. Further, it hinted that Steffen might succeed Whitmore as CEO. The article ended by quoting Steffen that being a Fortune 500 CEO "is certainly on the list of things I want to do."

No one anticipated the personality clash that would ensue. One can only speculate about the CEO's state of mind after reading about his possible replacement by an

---

19 See "Getting The Picture—Kodak Finally Heeds the Shareholders," *Business Week*, February 1, 1993, 24.

20 *Wall Street Journal*, April 28, 1993.

outsider who had worked for Kodak a mere three months. His reaction could be compared to a football player who diligently attended practice every day for years confronting a new star, who without much experience, believed he would save the team.

On Wednesday April 28, 1993, Steffen suddenly quit. The stock market reacted with panic. The opening of trading in Kodak stock was delayed thirteen minutes. On April 27, 1993, it had closed at $52⅜. The stock hit a low of $44 on April 28, 1993, before closing at $47¼. The front page of the local newspaper had two charts of the stock price. Steffen was quoted on the front page saying, "The company and I disagree on the approach to solving its problems."[21]

More than fifteen million shares traded on Wednesday, compared to its average daily volume of 1.35 million shares. Eighteen percent of the stock was owned by local shareholders.[22] Page 6A of the newspaper had another article with the headline, "Shareholders Described as 'Disgusted.'" The local newspaper repeated Whitmore's quote from the previous day's *Wall Street Journal* that, "If Chris Steffen comes in here assuming he's the Lone Ranger, he will not last very long."[23]

---

21 Rochester *Democrat and Chronicle*, Thursday, April 29, 1993, 1A.

22 Rochester *Democrat and Chronicle*, Thursday, April 29, 1993, 6A.

23 *The Wall Street Journal*, April 28, 1993, 1.

Steffen had lasted a mere 107 days : twenty days in January, twenty-eight days in February, thirty-one days in March, and twenty-eight days in April. But it was also the beginning of the end for CEO Whitmore. This debacle convinced the board that it was time for change at the very top.

While the specific reason or reasons for Steffen's departure were never fully disclosed, the financial press speculated that he had wanted to sell Sterling Drug, whose acquisition had been masterminded by CEO Whitmore. Also, it was reported that the board was slow to provide public support for CEO Whitmore.[24]

While investors waited for CEO Whitmore to disclose his action plan, Kodak continued to lose key executives specializing in electronics. It lost the architect of its Photo CD product and thirteen other workers in that area. It also lost a software vice president to Apple Computer.[25]

When his plan was finally announced it was perceived as too little and too late. The plan was to spin off Eastman Chemical to Eastman Kodak shareholders. This was actually accomplished on December 31, 1993, when Kodak paid a dividend to shareholders of one share of Eastman Chemical for every four shares of Eastman Kodak. When Kodak filed a bankruptcy petition approximately eighteen

---

24 "The Battle to Shape Up Kodak," *FORTUNE,* May 31, 1993, 63.

25 Business Section of Rochester *Democrat and Chronicle,* June 11, 1993, 10B.

years later, Eastman Chemical was a highly profitable corporation with its stock price near a record high. Had Kodak not spun off Eastman Chemical, it could have avoided bankruptcy. In the year ending 2011, Eastman Chemical earned a profit of more than $653 million.[26]

The spin-off did not address the Sterling Drug problem, the loss of market share to private label generic film, Kodak's bloated bureaucracy, or loss of key personnel in its Photo CD division. But if Kodak had really wanted to deconstruct its conglomerate business model, it should have sold Sterling Drug first. Moreover, financial analysts were still critical of Kodak's high debt load.[27]

The spin-off postponed any potential decision about layoffs and downsizing. This "Hamlet-like" indecision was the object of increasing attack in the financial press. "Company culture in need of shock" was the front page headline in the June 27, 1993, Rochester *Democrat and Chronicle.* "Why Kodak's Dazzling Spin-Off Didn't Bedazzle" was the title of an article in the June 28, 1993, issue of *Business Week.*

The shock would come unexpectedly on Friday, August 7, 1993. Kodak dismissed CEO Whitmore, and the price of a share of Kodak stock increased $3.25 to $58.625 on the New York Stock Exchange (NYSE). Residents of Rochester

---

26 *Value Line Investment Survey,* February 10, 2012, 2433.

27 See "Debt Still High, Analysts Wary,' in Rochester *Democrat and Chronicle,* June 17, 1993.

awoke to a front page headline in the *Democrat and Chronicle* on Saturday, August 6, 1993: "Kodak Ousts Whitmore; Shocks City, Drives Stock." The front page carried a large out-of-focus and overexposed color photograph of former CEO Whitmore with a grim frown on his face, as he drove his car away from 343 State Street after learning of his dismissal. The newspaper also had a sidebar entitled, "Pink Slip Pays Off." It calculated that the value of the soon-to-be ex-CEO's 28,700 shares of Kodak stock had increased in value by $93,274 to $1,682,537. In his official announcement, Whitmore said, "You can expect a new CEO to be brought in from outside the company."[28]

Rochester considered itself richer and superior to its upstate neighbors in Buffalo and Syracuse. Rochester had its own local telephone company, its own local gas and electric utility, and was the home of Xerox Corporation, whose dry copiers had revolutionized the business world. It was sometimes accused of having a narrow-minded outlook born of its past success and geographical isolation. "Some Wary of Outsider—New Chief Should Have Community Ties" was the headline of another article in the local newspaper that day.[29] In theory, the physical location or residence of a CEO should be irrelevant to his or her management abilities. After all, the for-

---

28 Rochester *Democrat and Chronicle*, Aug. 7, 1993, 7A.

29 Rochester *Democrat and Chronicle*, Aug. 7, 1993, 7A, top article.

mer CEO was a local resident—an insider. Why should local residency qualify a CEO? The article insinuated that an outsider might jeopardize Kodak's philanthropy. However, if Kodak continued its traditional practices, it might not have enough profits for any philanthropy. Perhaps the best change might be new blood—someone not tethered to the failures of the past. Someone with a history of turning around a troubled company, with the forward thinking sufficient to grasp the technological changes from chemical to electronic photography. In the spirit of Senator Barry Goldwater, who had proclaimed that extremism in defense of liberty is no vice, many residents of Rochester believed that xenophobia was a virtue.[30]

CEO Whitmore was in a no-win situation. If he had fired ten thousand Kodak workers, he would have been attacked as heartless and cruel. If he delayed the layoffs, he would have been criticized as a corporate Hamlet who could not make up his mind.

The axe fell on Kodak's workers twelve days after the announcement of CEO Whitmore's dismissal. In a letter to "Dear Fellow Employees," he announced that "On a worldwide basis we expect that 10,000 jobs will be eliminated by year-end 1995."[31]

---

30 For a post-bankruptcy opinion on the deleterious effect of geography see "Kodak Didn't Kill Rochester, It Was the Other Way Around," by Rich Karlgaard, in *The Wall Street Journal*, Jan. 13, 2012.

31 Rochester *Democrat and Chronicle*, Aug. 19, 1993, 10A.

The front page of the local newspaper on August 19, 1993, gave prominence to the effect of the layoffs on the market value of Kodak stock. It carried three blue-colored charts showing (1) "How Kodak stock performed yesterday," (2) "Weekly closing stock prices & volume" from January through August 18, 1993, and (3) "Weekly volume in millions of shares."[32] It typified the attitude of the "old money" Rochester that what really mattered was the price of Kodak stock. Under the front page headline "Announcement nudges stock," the paper stated that "Eastman Kodak Co.'s stock closed up 12.5 cents a share, after the company announced its debt-reduction plan."[33]

Question: Was the plan really a debt-reduction plan? Or was it a layoff plan? More important question: Should the readers sell their Kodak stock? The article put an optimistic spin in the 10,000 layoffs. It suggested that the stock would go up. "Area Can Absorb Layoffs" was the headline on page 11A. Included on that page were two other charts (in black and white, not blue), showing (1) "Kodak's shrinking labor force" and (2) "Rochester employment." Chart number two showed that at year end 1992 there were 39,300 people employed by Kodak in Rochester.[34]

---

32 Rochester *Democrat and Chronicle*, Thursday, Aug. 19, 1993, front page.

33 Rochester *Democrat and Chronicle*, Thursday, Aug., 19, 1993, front page.

34 Rochester *Democrat and Chronicle*, Aug. 19, 1993, 11A.

As if he were the sole cause of all Kodak's problems, the public criticism of CEO Whitmore was merciless, derogatory, intense, and sarcastic. That same day the local newspaper carried a cartoon with Whitmore's severed head pictured on a silver plate with the caption "ONLY 9,999 MORE TO GO..."Below the cartoon was an article by Richard Cohen entitled "In Japan, they don't lay off workers." Though it would be no consolation to the Kodak 10,000, later that year Xerox announced that it, too, would cut at least 10,000 jobs.[35] The Rochester economy was falling downhill.

On October 28, 1993, the Kodak board named its new CEO, who immediately tried to deal with demoralized employees by giving them an improvised pep talk.[36] George M. C. Fisher had a PhD in applied math, had joined Motorola in 1976, became its CEO in 1988, and led Motorola to an increase in profits at the dawn of the cellular telephone revolution.[37] On December 1, 1993, he officially became Kodak's CEO. Thus began the rational, methodical, and aggressive attempt to fix Kodak. If an executive with his education, record of prior achievements, and managerial skills could not fix Kodak, no one could.

---

35 *The Wall Street Journal*, Dec. 9, 1993.

36 See "Kodak: Shoot the Works," *Business Week*, Nov. 15, 1993, 30.

37 See "To: George Fisher—Re: How To Fix Kodak," *Business Week*, Nov. 8, 1993, 37.

Five days later Standard and Poor's lowered Kodak's debt ratings due to the impairment of cash flow caused by the Eastman Chemical spin-off.[38] Its senior debt rating was lowered from A- to BBB+.

---

38 *The Wall Street Journal,* Dec. 6, 1993.

4 - PRINTERLESS
(1993–1997)

The Kodak board tried to link the new CEO's pay to corporate performance. In addition to acquiring 107,400 shares at $63.19 per share, he was granted 20,000 shares of restricted stock, which required the new CEO to hold them for at least five years before being sold. Finally, he was granted options to buy 742,090 shares at $57.97 each, and options to buy 7,910 shares at $63.19 each, exercisable in 20 percent annual installments beginning in November of 1994.[39]

Implicit in such arrangements was the assumption that higher corporate profits would cause a higher price in Kodak stock.

Rochester's anxiety about its largest corporation being run by an outsider—not born, raised, schooled, or previously employed locally—was eased somewhat by the disclosure that the new CEO would buy a mansion on East Avenue. On May 19, 1994, George Fisher and his wife bought a 7,200 square foot residence on fourteen acres

---

39 Rochester *Democrat and Chronicle*, Dec. 17, 1993.

at number 4100 East Avenue in the Rochester suburb of Pittsford. The price was $2.35 million. The recently renovated house had maid and butler quarters.[40] Rochester residents could hope that "He's now one of us; he lives on the same street that George Eastman did."

Fisher began to rationalize Kodak's corporate structure. First, he made the electronic imaging unit separate and distinct from the chemical-based film unit (from which Kodak derived most of its profits). This would allow management and investors to monitor revenues, costs, cash flow, and earnings at the electronic unit and to measure its progress by hard numbers.[41] Second, he hired a new CFO, the former head of IBM's credit division, who proceeded to cut Kodak's debt by almost $1 billion in two months.[42] Third, and most important, on May 3, 1994, he announced that Kodak would sell its health care units to further reduce balance-sheet debt.[43]

On the same day that the local newspaper reported that "Israel, PLO to Sign Pact Today," the Rochester *Democrat and Chronicle* carried another front page story about the health-care divestitures. "Kodak Slims down for a 'War'" was the headline. As the Mideast edged

---

40 Rochester *Democrat and Chronicle*, May 20, 1994.

41 "Kodak to Reorganize Imaging Division to Emphasize Electronic Technology," *The Wall Street Journal*, February 24, 1994.

42 *Fortune*, May 16, 1994, 78.

43 *Business Week*, May 16, 1994, 32.

toward peace, Rochester prepared for the opposite. The newspaper quoted the CEO as saying that "A strategy that is not affordable is not a strategy. We at Kodak were trying to do too many things and, as a result, would probably end up not winning any war. This way, we'll end up winning the imaging war."[44]

The sale would include not only two divisions of the former Sterling Drug, but also Kodak's Clinical Diagnostics Division, which was founded in 1981 and employed 1000 workers in Rochester.[15] Kodak would henceforth devote most of its corporate energy to its central core business: photography. Healthcare, pharmaceuticals, and blood-testing equipment would no longer be distractions.

Kodak's prospects even improved in the courtroom. On May 20, 1994, the US District Court for the Western District of New York struck down as outdated two old consent decrees from 1921 and 1954 . The old decrees had prohibited Kodak from selling film with processing included.[46] The federal court's decision would also permit Kodak to enter the private label film market.

Finally, in 1994 Kodak began to study possible changes in employee compensation. The entire community knew that Kodak workers were over paid. No other local business could compete with Kodak's wages and benefits.

---

44 Rochester *Democrat and Chronicle*, May 4, 1994, front page.

45 Rochester *Democrat and Chronicle*, May 4, 1994, 9A

46 Rochester *Democrat and Chronicle*, Saturday, May 21, 1994, front page.

Even menial jobs, such as working on a loading dock, were highly paid. On the same day the local newspaper carried a front page story about the sale price for Sterling Winthrop, the biggest headline was: "Kodak to Tinker with Benefits." The new effort to link pay to performance would be from the top down. No one would automatically get a raise. A raise had to be earned by high performance.[47] The newspaper indicated that CEO Fisher wanted to measure company performance by return on net assets (net earnings divided by company average net assets). It also suggested that retirement benefits were under review. The article sent a collective shudder through Kodak's workers and retirees. The free ride was over.

Meanwhile, Kodak's systematic downsizing continued. On November 15, 1994, the company announced eight hundred layoffs at Kodak Park. The local newspaper ran an article about controlling stress. In a nonconfrontational milieu like Rochester, stress was seen as bad, never good. Among the advice provided by the newspaper were these: exercise, don't smoke or drink, don't use drugs, get support, and laugh.[48] Even though Rochester's manufacturing business was in decline, its local counseling business was in ascent. Psychologists, psychiatrists, and divorce lawyers would have increasingly lucrative prac-

---

47 Rochester *Democrat and Chronicle*, Tuesday, Aug. 30, 1994, front page

48 "Face job anxiety now, say area advisers," Rochester *Democrat and Chronicle*, Nov. 16, 1994, 8A.

tices. Divorce lawyers who could draft QDROs (Qualified Domestic Relations Orders) would be prominent speakers at local CLE (Continuing Legal Education) seminars.

By December 31, 1994, Kodak had sold most of its healthcare division for a total of $7,858 million. These discontinued businesses had sales of $3,175 million that year.[49] The sale proceeds reduced Kodak's debt from$7.5 billion to $1.5 billion.[50]

Can a great general win battles, no less wars, with mediocre soldiers and poor commanders? While a great general can create a superior strategy, it is the tactical commanders who implement that strategy on the ground. If they are not capable, the general's foresight comes to naught.

The fundamental problem the new CEO faced was a complacent, lethargic corporate culture inimical to change. " Decisions are too slow. People don't take risks," he was quoted as saying.[51] Speaking of Kodak's corporate culture, he stated,

"It was so hierarchically oriented that everybody looked to the guy above him for what needed to be

---

49 Eastman Kodak Company Form 10-K Annual Report for 1994, 4.
50 *Business Week*, Jan. 30, 1995, 63.
51 *Business Week*, Jan. 30, 1995, 63.

done....How can you hold a person accountable if you've had three overrides on his decision?[52]"

It was as if a man with the genius of General Patton commanded an army of sheep. The lack of initiative, resistance to change, fear of taking responsibility, living in the past, an exaggerated opinion of one's self-importance—the new CEO faced all these obstacles, and even more. Near the end of his first year in Rochester, how could the new CEO not be frustrated?[53]

The details of Kodak's changes to executive compensation were disclosed in the proxy statements for the 1995 annual meeting. The reforms centered on calculation of executive bonuses. Fifty percent would be based on shareholder satisfaction, 30 percent would be based on market-share growth, and 20 percent would be based on increasing the employment of women and minorities.[54]

Kodak tried to modernize its manufacturing competitiveness in three ways. First, it tried to increase quality control and reduce production time by posting daily updates to product defect rates and cycle times at the entrances to production facilities. Second, it tried to cure corporate lethargy by hiring digital and computer executives from outside the company. (This had the

---

52 *Business Week*, Jan. 30, 1995, 65.

53 See "Kodak under Fisher: Upheaval in Slow Motion," *The Wall Street Journal*, Dec 22, 1994, B1.

54 *The Wall Street Journal*, Mar. 13, 1995.

predictable effect of alienating the old guard of chemical-based imaging employees.)[55]Third, Kodak formed alliances and agreements with computer firms such as IBM and Microsoft.[56] Why reinvent the wheel? The alliances could shorten product development times and increase innovation.

In order to instill an aggressive fighting spirit into the company, the new CEO launched a legal war against its primary Japanese competitor, Fujifilm. On May 18, 1995, Kodak petitioned the US Trade Representative to investigate alleged illegal and unfair trade practices by its arch competitor. "Kodak Models Feistier Image" was the headline in the local newspaper. Underneath the main headline was a smaller headline in larger type: "Case Against Fuji Called a Daring, Aggressive Move."[57]In Japan, Kodak had a miniscule 9 percent of the market. Kodak attributed Fuji's 70 percent share of the Japanese market to its monopolistic control of film distribution. In the United States, film was distributed by manufacturers, but in Japan, Fuji allegedly controlled the four biggest film distributors. Kodak believed this closed distribution system was essentially a substitution for tariffs.[58]

55 See "George Fisher Pushes Kodak into Digital Era," *The Wall Street Journal*, June 9, 1995.

56 See "Kodak, Taking the Digital Plunge, Will Line up with Computer Giants," *The New York Times*, April 3, 1995.

57 Rochester *Democrat and Chronicle*, June 1, 1995.

58 *Business Week*, July 10, 1995; *The Wall Street Journal*, "Kodak Case Against Japan Is Stronger Than That of Auto Firms, Analysts Say," June 9, 1995.

This case must be understood in the context of the times. Japan was then seen as the number one competitor to American companies. The Ministry of International Trade and Industry (MITI) was often accused of targeting whole American industries, such as automobile and semiconductor manufacturing. The onslaught of products from Japan and the inability of American companies to penetrate the Japanese home market was referred to as "Japan, Inc." It had succeeded in driving Intel Corporation out of the Dynamic Random Access Memory (DRAM) business, while Japanese automobiles were of higher quality and used less gasoline than their American counterparts.

Fuji countered with a 585-page report entitled "Rewriting History," accusing Kodak of hypocrisy in monopolizing its home market in the United States.[59]

As the year progressed, Kodak's electronic strategy started to gather strength. Kodak became the largest American producer of electronic imaging sensors known as charge-coupled devices (CCDs).[60] It introduced a six megapixel digital camera that cost $28,000.[61] Though its Photo CD had failed with consumers, it was a success with businesses. Kodak introduced an open architecture, offering free licensing for the software that converted

59 *The Wall Street Journal,* July 30, 1995.
60 *Business Week,* Mar. 6, 1995, 55.
61 *Forbes,* Mar. 27, 1995, 118.

photos in digital images on the Photo CDs.[62] It sought to set the future standards for the industry by dominating it from the beginning. The Fisher "open architecture" strategy was the polar opposite of the future Perez intellectual property "monetize through lawsuit" strategy, which would become the basis of Kodak's profits shortly before its bankruptcy.

The coming incredible collapse of the Rochester economy was foreshadowed on October 8, 1995, when Section 3 of the Sunday edition of *The New York Times* carried a front page article entitled "A Doting Uncle Cuts Back, and a City Feels the Pain—Kodak Rethinks Its Civic Duties in Rochester."[63] It highlighted how Kodak cut its charitable contributions from $20 million in 1988 to $13 million in 1994. More ominously, it reported how Kodak threatened to increase health-care costs in the local community by using its market power to negotiate lower premiums for its own employees. This would mean that non-Kodak workers would pay higher rates for essentially the same health care. This was the beginning of the upward spiral in the cost of local health-care insurance. In 1995 no one had any real idea of how high health insurance would eventually cost. No one can serve two masters, and clearly it was in Kodak's pure self-interest to reduce health-care premiums for its own employees.

---

62 *Fortune*, May 1, 1995, 82.

63 See *Money and Business*, Section, 1.

For analytical purposes it is useful to benchmark 1995, as this was the first year that Kodak was essentially a photography company. Gone were Lysol and Bayer aspirin, gone was Eastman Chemical, and gone were blood analyzers. As of year-end 1995, Kodak employed 96,600 worldwide and employed 54,400 in the United States.[64] Its 1995 sales were $14,980 million and its earnings were $3.67 per share or $1,252 million.[65]

Under the Heading "Research and Development" the very last sentence on page four of the 1995 Form 10-K stated,

> While in the aggregate Kodak's patents are considered to be of material importance in the operation of its business, *it does not consider that the patents relating to any single product or process are of* material significance *when judged from the standpoint of its total business.*[66] [emphasis added]

Nothing was said in the 1995 Form 10-K about the longevity or remaining lives or expiration of patents. Fifteen years in the future Kodak's Form 10-K would indeed emphasize its patents:

> The Company's major products are not dependent upon one single, material patent. Rather, the

---

64 Eastman Kodak Co., Form 10-K annual report for the year ended Dec. 31, 1995, 5.

65 Ibid, 11.

66 Ibid, 4.

technologies that underlie the Company's products are supported by an aggregation of patents having various remaining lives and expiration dates. There is no individual patent expiration or group of patents expirations which are expected to have a material impact of the Company's results of operations.[67]

For Kodak, 1996 would be the year of the APS Camera (Advanced Photo System). This was supposed to be the transition between traditional chemical-based film photography and the new filmless electronic world. It was designed to prolong the film business until Kodak's new electronic photography business was ready. Created by Kodak, its arch-rival Fuji, and three other Japanese camera manufacturers, it was announced with great fanfare simultaneously in Rochester, Tokyo, and Los Angeles on February 1, 1996. Local guests at the George Eastman House danced and drank champagne after CEO Fisher's televised introduction of the APS camera.[68] The APS negative was about 60 percent of the size of a 35mm negative and was made on a new kind of film base.[69] It was hoped the new film base would avoid the graininess problems of the Disc system. Electronically, the camera was truly advanced. Each negative was associated with a distinct number, making it easier for photofinishers

---

67 Eastman Kodak Co., Form 10-K annual report for the year ended Dec. 31, 2010, 7.

68 Rochester *Democrat and Chronicle, Feb. 1, 1996,* 6A.

69 Rochester *Democrat and Chronicle,* Feb. 1, 1996, 7A.

to print. Spooling and unspooling of the film was done automatically, negatives were stored inside the film cartridge, and mid-roll changes of film cartridges were possible. For example, a consumer could change from a 100 speed film to a 400 speed film in the middle of a roll. The back of the camera had an LCD panel showing the date each photo was taken. The processed cartridges were returned with an index print, showing a small picture of each photograph, making it easier to reorder prints.[70]

Unfortunately, not even all the management changes in the last three years could restrain Kodak from engaging in its typical corporate hubris. Kodak touted the APS System as "the most significant consumer product introduction in 30 years." [71] Was it really more important than the personal computer, the laser printer, or the Internet? Was APS really the Next Big Thing? Within ten short years, the legacy of the APS System would be the APS-sized image sensors common to many Japanese digital cameras. By 2010 it would be almost impossible to buy an APS film cartridge. No one on that first day of February 1996, anticipated the rapid decline of chemical film imaging. Furthermore, it was highly unlikely that advanced amateurs and professionals would abandon their 35mm cameras for a camera without interchangeable lenses. In terms of preventing the inevitable decline

70 Rochester *Democrat and Chronicle*, Feb. 1, 1996, 6A.

71 Rochester *Democrat and Chronicle*, Feb. 1, 1996, 6A.

of film, with the benefit of hindsight, the APS Camera cannot be judged a success.

The inability to anticipate the rapid rise of digital photography was exemplified by the extraordinarily high prices for digital cameras in 1996. Kodak's professional digital camera, the NC 2000E, had a sensor with 1.3 megapixels and sold for $15,250. Its business/consumer digital camera, the DC50, had a resolution of 380,000 pixels and sold for $980.[72] How could such high-priced cameras be popular with ordinary consumers?

By the end of 1996 it looked like Kodak's turnaround was for real. Its annual sales increased 7 percent, and its earnings per share increased 4 percent.[73] Its once-moribund stock price, which had been as low as $47¼ in 1995, hit a high of $85 in the fourth quarter of 1996.[74]

Even the once-skeptical financial press published articles praising Kodak. The January 13, 1997 issue of *Forbes* magazine carried a story entitled "How an Outsider's Vision Saved Kodak." Forgetting the old adage about counting chickens before they hatched, and in the spirit of the "Mission Accomplished" sign that once greeted former Pres. George W. Bush, the article featured a large color photograph of the new CEO holding an old folding camera in his left hand and a newer camera at a higher

---

72 *Business Week*, April 15, 1996, 72.

73 Eastman Kodak Co., Form 10-K annual report for the year ended Dec. 31, 1996, 11.

74 Ibid, 11.

level in his right hand, juxtaposed against a background of a large white window in front of a blue sky. The symbolism was unmistakable. It also featured two other color photographs of smiling executives.[75] The article ended with this statement by Fisher: "Success to me in this company is not only getting a financially healthy and growing company again—it's also having arrived at the day that I can leave here and this place can run as well without me as it can with me."[76]

Kodak was indeed then financially healthy and growing again. But what would happen if and when CEO Fisher left? Would his successors have the same managerial abilities to formulate and execute strategy and to achieve realistic objectives? Daniel Carp, whose picture also appeared in the *Forbes* article, was designated president and chief operating officer. He was being groomed for the transition to Kodak's next CEO.

The first inkling that 1997 would not end as well as it began occurred on February 16, 1997. The local newspaper carried a large headline at the very top of its Sunday edition: "Digital Giant Challenges Kodak." The paper announced that on March 17, 1997, Hewlett-Packard, the giant computer company, would announce a full digital product line to compete against Kodak. Its PhotoSmart system would include a $399 digital camera, a printer,

---

75 *Forbes Magazine*, Jan. 13, 1997, 45–47.
76 Ibid, 47.

and a scanner.[77] This time the competition would not be from Japan; it would be from California. The competition would be from the giant innovative computer company that had created Silicon Valley.

The full extent of Hewlett-Packard's threat became apparent several months afterward. The July 7, 1997, issue of *Business Week* had a front page photograph of the CEO of Hewlett-Packard holding a flashing digital camera. The article was entitled "SHOOTOUT!—How HP Plans to Take on Kodak—And Revolutionize the Way You Capture and Print Images." Hewlett-Packard's strategy was to eliminate commercial and independent photofinishers, as well as photofinishers in drugstores and grocery stores. It hoped to create a home or office-based digital darkroom, dominated by its very own printers and scanners. Kodak, the article correctly argued, had no home digital printer.[78] (Kodak's failure to make or market a computer printer was the digital equivalent of the Insterburg Gap in East Prussia, through which the Czar's armies would try to attack and destroy the Kaiser's armies in World War I.[79]) HP hoped to use the Internet to enable consumers to send photographs electronically to other computers, bypassing the old-fashioned custom of sending photographs by "snail" mail.

---

77 Rochester *Democrat and Chronicle*, Sunday, February 16, 1997, 1.

78 *Business Week*, July 7, 1997, 102.

79 *The Guns of August*, Barbara W. Tuchman, 318.

Question: Why, in the approximately three years since George Fisher had become CEO, did Kodak not make or market a computer printer? Before Kodak would file for bankruptcy in 2012, the computer printer was its principal product. Hewlett-Packard planned to invest $7.5 billion in computer printers from 1997 through 2000.[80]

Taking a cue from Kodak's own "razor blade" strategy of profiting not from the cameras but from the film, Hewlett-Packard hoped to profit not from the printers, but from the paper and toner cartridges.[81] The article cited then "Inkjet chief Antonio M. Perez" vowing to triple Hewlett-Packard's inkjet printers to 150 by the year 2000.[82]

Hewlett-Packard had identified the major flaw in Kodak's digital strategy, and had attacked that flaw. The old nightmare about Kodak's survival in the digital age, which had slowly faded away, suddenly reemerged with a vengeance. Could CEO Fisher save Kodak? Those who had praised the new CEO for saving Kodak seemed to have forgotten the ancient warning about crowning the victor with laurel before the race is finished. For the year 1997 culminated in massive layoffs.

The first harbinger of disaster came with the release of Kodak's second quarter results. While it was the third

---

80 *Business Week*, July 7, 1997, 102.

81 Ibid, 103.

82 Ibid, 106.

quarter in a row of declining profits, what really disturbed analysts was the disclosure that to date in 1997 Kodak lost more than $100 million on digital products.[83] Additionally, Rochester natives were reported to be upset with CEO Fisher's head of marketing, who refused to move to Rochester.[84]

The local newspaper had an interview with the head of Kodak's Digital and Applied Imaging Division (DA&I). In the interview he explained the short life cycle of digital cameras. Kodak's DC40 introduced in 1995 became obsolete in only two years. Its then current DC120 had a one megapixel sensor and retailed for $999.[85] Within approximately two weeks of that interview, he suddenly resigned. He had lasted only seventeen months.[86]

Investors would start to panic in September. After the close of trading on the NYSE on September 15, 1997, Kodak issued a press release that 1997 earnings could decline by at least 25 percent. Kodak's stock, which had been over $90 per share early in 1997, declined by $5.50 to close at $60 on September 15, 1997.[87] It was also reported that Fujifilm was building a new film production plant in South Carolina and was "stealing" US

---

83 *The Wall Street Journal,* July 25, 1997, A1 and A6.

84 Ibid, A6.

85 Rochester *Democrat and Chronicle,* July 28, 1997.

86 *The Wall Street Journal,* Aug. 8, 1997.

87 Rochester *Democrat and Chronicle,* Sept. 16, 1997, A1.

market share from Kodak.[88] CEO Fisher issued a written statement that Kodak was "under siege." He also blamed Fuji for "exploiting its profit sanctuary in Japan" and claimed to be disadvantaged by a "strong US dollar." He added that,"Over the next few weeks and months, we will take further actions to strengthen our competitiveness along the lines stated in this letter..."[89]

While the statement itself did not give specifics about the further actions, it was also reported that in May, the CEO had exercised 300,000 of his stock options for $9 million.[90] Although there was nothing irregular or improper about this, its disclosure antagonized other investors who held their stock and watched it fall in value.

During its September 16, 1997, conference call with analysts, Kodak acknowledged pricing pressure and loss of market share to Fuji.[91] The CEO acknowledged there would be layoffs.[92]

The new layoffs began on September 26, 1997, when Kodak announced it would fire two hundred high-level executives, and 10 percent of its support staff.[93] For the

---

88 Ibid, 9A.

89 Rochester *Democrat and Chronicle*, Sept . 16, 1997, 8A.

90 See "Investor Reaction—'I'm Not Going to Run Away Scared'," Rochester *Democrat and Chronicle*, Sept. 16, 1997, 8A.

91 *The Wall Street Journal*, Sept. 17, 1997.

92 Ibid.

93 Rochester *Democrat and Chronicle*, Sept. 26, 1997, 1.

very first time in memory, Kodak would lay off employees in research and development. Kodak's announcement, jointly signed by George Fisher and Dan Carp, spoke of the R&D reductions as follows:

> Our actions in R&D will be portfolio driven in two respects. First, R&D investment will no longer be needed as we exit business segments or product lines. Second, we will take a much more focused approach to growth opportunities. The result will be a reduction in R&D support for some areas in order to strengthen efforts in the areas of highest potential.[94]

Until this time, R&D had always been sacred at Kodak. The Empire was recalling its legions. No one knew where the retreat would end. How could Kodak win the war if it reduced its R&D on weapons?

What Kodak had touted as "the most significant consumer product introduction in 30 years"[95] had a troubled introduction. Kodak didn't make enough APS cameras or processing equipment for photofinishers. The whole product line would have to be relaunched.[96]

Kodak's CEO had cited Niccolo Macchiavelli's *The Prince* in a 1995 speech to employees.[97] He did not cite,

---

94 Rochester *Democrat and Chronicle,* Sept. 26, 1997, 14A.

95 See footnote 71.

96 *Fortune,* Oct. 27, 1997, 188.

97 *Business Week,* Jan. 30, 1996, 68.

however, the closing lines of Chapter Eight of *The Prince* that injuries or cruelties should be done all at once.[98] He had waited almost four years since becoming CEO before announcing massive layoffs. Not only were the layoffs not done all at once, they were done with increasing orders of magnitude. It was as if the guillotine had been abandoned in favor of the death of one thousand cuts. The second 1997 restructuring would be almost fifty times the size of the first.

"Kodak Cuts 10,000 Jobs," screamed the headline of the local newspaper. To the right of the headline was a quotation by CEO Fisher in large red letters: "We are collectively embarrassed by this year."[99]

Through the first nine months of 1997, Kodak lost $300 million in its digital imaging business.[100] Kodak would take a $1 billion charge in the fourth quarter to pay for the cost-cutting. Earnings for 1997 would decline to about $1 per share.[101] On November 11, 1997, Kodak stock declined $4.06 on the NYSE. The restructuring sought $1 billion in cost savings. Research and Development (R&D)

---

98 See *The Prince*, by Niccolo Machiavelli, translated by Christian Gauss, based on translation by Luigi Ricci, The New American Library of World Literature, published as a Mentor Book, 15th printing, 1964; also *MACBETH*, Act I, Sc. VII: "*If it were done when 'tis done, then 'twere well It were done quickly.*"

99 Rochester *Democrat and Chronicle*, Nov. 12 1997, A1.

100 Ibid.

101 Ibid, 11A.

would suffer a cut in its 1998 budget of approximately between $100 million to $150 million.[102]

The new cuts caused employee morale to sink.[103] The local newspaper reported that "Investors Turn Thumbs Down" and carried a chart of the declining stock price on the front page.[104] What the general public did not then know was that even more cuts were to come later in 1997. In fact, Wall Street had been lobbying for layoffs twice as large.[105] Wall Street's wish would soon be granted.

Despite pressure from Wall Street for 20,000 layoffs, CEO Fisher publicly maintained that 10,000 positions would be cut worldwide and that Kodak intended to be humane and compassionate.[106] The financial press questioned Kodak's strategy of installing thousands of digital print stations in retail stores instead of creating the digital darkroom of computers, software, and digital printers.[107] On the other hand, he came under attack in the local newspaper for favoring Wall Street over Kodak

---

102 Ibid, 11A.

103 See "Many Say Morale Sinks as the Job-cutting Ax Hangs over Heads," Rochester *Democrat and Chronicle,* Nov. 12, 1997, 11A.

104 Rochester *Democrat and Chronicle,* Nov. 12, 1997, A1.

105 See *Business Week,* Oct. 20, 1997, 118.

106 See "Speaking Out" page article by George M. C. Fisher—"At Issue: Kodak Restructuring—Slogging through Mud to Reach High Ground," Rochester *Democrat and Chronicle,* Nov. 16, 1997, 27A.

107 See "Kodak's Focus May Be Too Narrow," *Business Week,* Nov. 24, 1997, 42.

employees. It was even suggested that he return part of his salary, together with other top executives.[108]

Wall Street prevailed, and on December 18, 1997, Kodak announced that job cuts would climb to 19,900 by the end of 1999. The total job cuts in the Rochester area during that period would be 6,300, which was 18.5 percent of Kodak's 34,000 local workers.[109]

In an interview with the local newspaper the next day, the CEO asserted that "10,000 (jobs) was a good estimate."[110]

He also defended his compensation as fair and reasonable. He correctly pointed out that his two million stock options would be worthless unless Kodak's share price exceeded $90.125; on December 18, 1997, it was $58.[111] It rose $1.50 on the day Kodak announced the increased number of layoffs. It was almost inevitable that, like his predecessor, he would be the subject of personal attacks in the local media. He was accused of sacrificing workers to profits and causing employees to cry. He was attacked for making Kodak weaker.[112]

---

108 See "Fisher Should Reassure Kodak Workers, Not Just Wall Street Traders," Rochester *Democrat and Chronicle*, Nov. 14, 1997.

109 Rochester *Democrat and Chronicle*, Dec. 19, 1997.

110 Ibid, 1A.

111 Ibid.

112 Rochester *Democrat and Chronicle*, "Is George Fisher Drawn to Siren Call of Shortsighted Analysts?" Dec. 19, 1997.

Late 1993 was the time for a real photographer to lead Kodak. He or she should have realized the importance of digital imaging software for personal computers and the need for a color inkjet printer to process those images. He or she should have realized that consumers preferred to print their images in the comfort and privacy of their own homes, as opposed to driving to a store, finding a place to park, waiting in line, and using a digital kiosk there. It was simply more convenient and less hassle to print digital photos at home with a personal computer and color inkjet printer. In the age of the digital darkroom, a digital kiosk in a retail store would become unnecessary.

The merger of Kodak's digital imaging group with a major software or hardware company never happened. One can only speculate why CEO Fisher did not push for a merger between his former employer Motorola and Kodak's DA&I group. Most photographs would eventually be taken with cell phones. Kodak might still be around in 2012 had it merged with Motorola and transferred its imaging technology to cell phones.

Expectations for a turnaround had been unrealistically high. Since 1982, when Kodak had employed 60,406 workers in Rochester, local employment shrank to 34,400 in 1997, and was scheduled to reach 28,100 by 1999.[113] The Mayor of Rochester evidently had not been

---

113 Rochester *Democrat and Chronicle*, Dec. 19, 1997, 15A.

informed in advance of the increased job cuts. He called the method "inappropriate."[114] Several R&D engineers learned of the cuts as they gathered for their Christmas lunch.[115]

---

114 Ibid.

115 Ibid.

5 - FISHER TO CARP
(1998–1999)

In Rochester, the year 1998 would be remembered as the Year of the Layoffs. The full fury of Kodak layoffs struck that year. The 1997 Form 10-K set forth the details of the worldwide layoffs. In addition to the 2000 employees remaining to be cut under the 1996 restructuring and the 800 remaining to be cut under the restructuring in the second quarter of 1997,[116] the following worldwide layoffs were to be completed in 1998:

(1) Manufacturing Facilities: 7,950.
(2) Services and Photofinishing: 2,675.
(3) Sales and Marketing: 1,425.
(4) R&D: 1,000.
(5) Administrative: 3,050.[117]

TOTAL	*16,100*

The timing of the latest restructuring announcement in the midst of the Christmas and New Year's holiday season contributed to growing community pessimism. There

---

116 Eastman Kodak Company, Form 10-K annual report for the year ended Dec. 31, 1997, 12.

117 Ibid, 38.

were complaints of betrayal, undignified treatment, and loss of benefits.[118] It did not help that in December, 1997, the World Trade Organization ruled against Kodak.[119]

For 1997, Kodak's earnings from operations declined 93 percent from $1.845 billion to only $130 million.[120] The CEO received no bonus that year.[121] Kodak's stock price had declined. Management was under intense pressure to show real results. When would the layoffs produce those results?

At first the bad news continued. Kodak's much-hyped Advanced Photo System, which had suffered from lack of cameras to lack of photofinishing equipment, suffered an additional embarrassment: manufacturing defects. Of the two million APS cameras made by Kodak in 1997, approximately 20,000 had defective shutters. Kodak spent almost $1 million to recall the cameras and correct the problem.[122]

Eventually the APS system became popular with consumers and photofinishers. By almost the end of 1997, Kodak estimated that APS cameras had about 30 percent

---

118 See "The Kodak Lesson: Forget Loyalty; Look out for No. 1," Rochester *Democrat and Chronicle,* Jan. 14, 1998, 7A.

119 *Business Week,* April 6, 1998, 38.

120 Eastman Kodak Co., Form 10-K annual report for the year ended Dec. 31, 1997, 10.

121 *Business Week,* April 6, 1998, 37.

122 *The Wall Street Journal,* April 28, 1998.

of the US market for camera sales, and about 8 percent of the US market for film sales.[123]

Kodak continued to collaborate with leading technology companies. The head of Kodak's digital unit announced a cross-licensing agreement with Intel Corporation involving all digital camera patents of both companies.[124] It also accelerated its push into rapidly growing emerging markets. Kodak was chosen to restructure three domestic Chinese photography companies, and invest possibly $1 billion into them.[125]

By the time it announced its second quarter 1998 earnings, the cost cuts and joint ventures had helped increase Kodak's profit margins from 10.7 percent to 15.6 percent.[126] Its second quarter earnings increased 35 percent over 1997.[127] Its domestic market share of the film market stabilized at 73 percent.[128] The stock market was willing to overlook the 8 percent decline in Kodak's sales.[129] For a few brief months, Kodak had a respite from bad news.

---

123 See "For New Film, a Brighter Picture," *The Wall Street Journal,* May 5, 1998, B1.

124 *The Wall Street Journal,* May 1, 1998.

125 *Fortune,* May 11, 1998, 180.

126 *Forbes,* Sept. 7, 1998, 65.

127 *Business Week,* July 27, 1998, 34.

128 *The Wall Street Journal,* Oct. 8, 1998.

129 *Business Week,* July 27, 1998, 34.

The horror show resumed when Kodak announced its third quarter 1998 earnings. Although its earnings increased more than 70 percent to $391 million, its sales declined 10 percent.[130] On October 13, 1998, Kodak's stock price on the NYSE declined $11.19 to $72.38.[131] Investors large and small had finally realized that although profits increased, the company was not growing. Sales had declined for seven quarters in a row.[132]

Kodak's 1998 annual report filed with the Securities and Exchange Commission made abundantly clear how the cost-cutting had increased earnings. Sales for 1998 decreased 8 percent from 1997, but earnings per share increased to $4.30 from $.01 the year before.[133] Total worldwide employment in 1998 decreased from 97,500 at the end of 1997 to 86,200 at the end of 1998.[134] R&D expenditures decreased from $1,230 million in 1997 to $922 million in 1998.[135] Meanwhile gross profit margins increased from 44.5 percent in 1997 to 45.6 percent in 1998.[136] Kodak reduced its operating costs in 1998 by

---

130 Rochester *Democrat and Chronicle,* Oct. 14, 1998, A1.

131 Ibid.

132 Ibid.

133 Eastman Kodak Company, Form 10-K annual report for the year ended Dec. 31, 1998, 11.

134 Ibid, 6.

135 Ibid, 6.

136 Ibid, 14.

approximately $730 million, including approximately $95 million in lower pension and healthcare costs.[137]

More information was disclosed about the company's plans in China. Kodak intended to invest more than $1 billion in China over several years.[138] In February 1998, Kodak contributed $308 million to Kodak (China) Company Limited (KCCL), and $32 million to Kodak (Wuxi) Company Limited KWCL.[139]

Kodak was about to commit another fundamental strategic mistake. It had, in the recent past, stopped making 35mm cameras just before the 35mm market was to explode, wasted untold monies and time plagiarizing Polaroid instant cameras, and wrongly diversified into the drug and household products industries. And now Kodak was to throw away $1 billion on a new film plant in China, almost in time for film to be rendered obsolete by digital cameras.

Kodak believed that in 1997 Chinese consumers bought about 170 million rolls of film and that China would soon become the world's largest market for photographic film.[140]

---

137 Ibid, 15.

138 Ibid, 16.

139 Ibid, 58, Note 15.

140 See "Not Made in Rochester," Rochester *Democrat and Chronicle*, Aug. 1, 1999, 2E.

In China Kodak would build its first new photographic film plant in almost thirty years. This was part of the previously disclosed $1 billion investment in China. Kodak expected the new plant to produce 100 million rolls of photographic film each year.[141]

Such a large capital expenditure on old technology in a foreign country exemplifies Kodak's conviction that photographic film would have a long and prosperous future. That $1 billion investment could have been used to purchase a software company in Silicon Valley, to increase R&D on American digital products, or to construct a factory to build digital cameras. Why could Kodak not simply have exported film from Rochester to China? One answer is to avoid Chinese film tariffs. A more intriguing answer is that Kodak intended to transfer film production from higher cost factories in Rochester to lower cost factories in China in order to facilitate additional layoffs in Rochester. The substitution of Chinese film production in place of Rochester film production could materially lower Kodak's costs. Chinese wages would be lower than Rochester wages, and there would be minimal, if any, health-care costs and pension costs for Chinese workers. In short, the massive investment in Chinese film production raised suspicions that Kodak would transform Rochester, New York, into Pontiac, Michigan. No one really knows if this

---

141 Ibid.

was Kodak's motivation, but the possibility cannot be ruled out or criticized as paranoia.

By the middle of 1999 the financial press voiced increasing worries about Kodak's future. In particular, Kodak's decision to slash R&D spending came under attack.[142] The 1998 Form 10-K had disclosed $308 million cuts in annual R&D spending.[143] Analysts worried that Kodak was reducing R&D spending on digital products. Others worried about CEO Fisher's exit on December 31, 1999.[144] While CEO Fisher had greatly improved Kodak's finances, analysts estimated that Kodak would continue to lose money on its digital products in 1999.[145]

Foreshadowing things to come, Kodak suddenly closed its Elmgrove plant in the Rochester suburb of Gates. The plant had opened in 1967, and contained 14 buildings on 770 acres of land. In a single stroke, Kodak destroyed about 20 percent of the property tax base of the Town of Gates, laid off 1,300 employees, and doubled the vacant industrial space in Monroe County.[146] This, apparently, was done with no advance notice to local politicians.[147] It was never publicly stated by Kodak that the closure

---

142 See "The Picture Just Keeps Getting Darker at Kodak,' *Fortune*, June 21, 1999, 206.

143 See footnote 135, supra.

144 See "Fisher's Photo Finish," *Business Week*, June 21, 1999, 34.

145 Ibid, 35.

146 Rochester *Democrat and Chronicle*, July 22, 1999, 1A and 6A.

147 Ibid.

of Elmgrove was part of a plan to transfer production to China. In fact, Kodak would relocate 4,500 remaining Elmgrove workers to Kodak Park in Rochester.[148] However, the concentration of Kodak employees in one location made it easier to fire them (when the time was appropriate).

Analysis of Kodak's actions reveals that (1) it had downsized its domestic operations, (2) expanded its Chinese operations, and (3) tried to establish a critical mass in digital products.

Kodak's 1999 efforts to establish the critical mass in digital products took several directions. First, it changed the name of its "Photo CD" to "Picture CD." Whenever a consumer had a roll of film developed, for an additional charge of $10 the photofinisher would scan the images onto a CD. (This cost was one-half the cost of doing the same thing with a "Photo CD.") The consumer could insert the CD into a personal computer, manipulate the images, or even e-mail them over the Internet.[149] Unfortunately, the Picture CD would cannibalize the market for Kodak's Photo Kiosks. Why go to a retail store to use a Photo Kiosk if you could do the same thing at home with a personal computer? In 1999 there was still no Kodak digital inkjet printer.

---

148 Ibid.

149 *Forbes*, July 26, 1999, 254.

On August 12, 1999, Kodak introduced the Quick Print program. Without using personal computers, consumers could upload images from their Kodak digital cameras directly to an Internet website, where they could purchase prints.[150] It seems not to have occurred to Kodak that it might be easier, quicker, and less expensive for consumers to print their images on their own inkjet printers.

That same day, Kodak continued its forced march into digital photography with the introduction of three new camera models. The lowest priced model, the DC215, had a 1.3 megapixel sensor and price of $399. The highest priced model, the DC290, had a 2.1 megapixel sensor and a price of $1,099.[151] By current measures both cameras now seem vastly overpriced. At about this time, Kodak was a distant number two in US digital camera sales. Kodak had a 17 percent share of the market, but Sony Corp. had a 52 percent share.[152]

Rochester's bad luck would not end. Just in time for the holiday season, another large local employer announced massive layoffs. On December 1, 1999, the CEO of Bausch & Lomb announced it would lay off 25 percent of its local workforce. The company would let go

---

150 See "Digital Photo, Traditional Print," Rochester *Democrat and Chronicle*, Aug. 13, 1999, 12D.

151 Ibid.

152 *Business Week*, Aug. 2, 1999 , p66 et seq.

600 people locally, part of a company-wide reduction of 850 workers.[153]

In this local atmosphere of anxiety and hurt feelings, Fisher reflected on his record as Kodak's CEO in a newspaper interview. He had restored Kodak's financial health, streamlined its management, and forced it to embrace digital technology, while enhancing its traditional business by introducing the APS camera and film. The local newspaper mentioned that Kodak's stock closed at $64.56 on December 28, 1999, but had been much higher earlier in Fisher's tenure. It also published reports suggesting he had been pushed out by a fed-up board.[154] In the interview, the reporter asked derogatory questions such as "Do you feel you've failed?"[155] Without his reforms, Kodak would have been mired in debt and unable to concentrate on photography due to the distraction of managing Sterling Drug. The real failure would come about twelve years later, when Kodak would file a Petition for bankruptcy. Fisher in no way can be held accountable for that. He prolonged the very sick patient's life; when the physicians changed, the patient got sicker and died.

---

153 Rochester *Democrat and Chronicle*, Dec. 2, 1999, 1A

154 See "Fisher Defends Record at Kodak," Rochester *Democrat and Chronicle*, Dec. 29, 1999, 12D.

155 Ibid.

Fisher would be succeeded as CEO on January 1, 2000, by Daniel Carp. The local newspaper noted that the new CEO would take office a year before Fisher's contract ended on December 31, 2000.[156] Fisher would remain chairman of the board until then.

When George Fisher became Kodak's new CEO near the end of 1993, Eastman Kodak Company had a loss per share of $4.62[157] and had long-term debt of $6.853 billion.[158] When he left the CEO position near the end of 1999, Eastman Kodak Company had earnings per share of $4.33[159] and had long-term debt of only $936 million. He had left the company in a stronger financial position than when he found it.

---

156 Ibid.

157 Eastman Kodak Company, Form 10-K annual report for the year ended Dec. 31, 1993, 9.

158 Ibid, 10.

159 Eastman Kodak Company, Form 10-K annual report for the year ended Dec. 31, 1999, 30.

6 - NEW MILLENNIUM, OLD KODAK
(2000–2005)

As the year 2000 began, the stock market entered the final phase of the tech bubble. On Monday, March 13, 2000, as the NASDAQ climbed past the 5000 level, the new CEO of Kodak gave an interview in the local newspaper. He criticized Kodak's health-care costs, emphasized his commitment to diversity, argued against unionization of Kodak's workforce, and spoke of increasing productivity at Kodak Park.[160]

He was not asked about Kodak's internal forecast for market share of film versus digital in 2010. In 1990 Kodak's forecast had been 30 percent for digital photography.[161] By the year 2000, there were other predictions. Japanese camera maker Sanyo estimated that in ten years film would completely disappear.[162] One of the

---

160 See "A Talk with the New CEO—Taking Kodak into the New-tech World," Rochester *Democrat and Chronicle*, March 13, 2000, 5F.

161 See note 8, supra.

162 *Forbes*, March 20, 2000, 80.

founders of Internet pioneer Netscape Communications predicted that film would die in four years.[163]

In the face of the growing digital threat to kill film, Kodak's response was to plow doggedly ahead, reemphasizing the importance of film. For example, Kodak's ads for the Sydney Olympics promoted only film and no digital products.[164] Also, Kodak gave high priority to its new film factory in China.

From 1995 to 2000, Kodak's workforce in China expanded from 316 to 5,556.[165] The new film plant in Xiamen, which had been designed and built with the help of Kodak Park employees, included almost 1.4 million square feet. It had cost approximately $600 million to build. Local Chinese workers worked a forty-hour week there.[166] Some Kodak Park workers worried they would be replaced by lower paid Chinese workers.[167] Kodak sought to take full advantage of its second-largest market, where its market share in 1999 was 40 percent.[168]

If film were going to be killed by digital in four to ten years, then why spend so much money building a new film plant and hiring thousands of foreign workers?

---

163 See *Red Herring*, July 24, 2000.

164 *Business Week*, Oct. 9, 2000, 52.

165 Rochester *Democrat and Chronicle*, "The New China," 1.

166 Ibid, 3.

167 Ibid, 3.

168 Ibid, 3.

Perhaps viewing China as a Lesser Developed Country (LDC), Kodak never believed that its second largest market would adopt the newest technology as rapidly as the rest of the world. Alternatively, Kodak could have been in denial about the imminent destruction of the film market.

The state of denial was apparent in the September 26, 2000, earnings conference call. Kodak reduced its third quarter earnings guidance by twenty to twenty-five cents below its previous guidance, which amounted to a reduction of about 15 percent. It also warned it might have to reduce its fourth quarter guidance. Kodak's chief financial officer said he could not fully explain the September slump.[169] Once again Kodak stock suffered a massive decline, by falling $14.40 to $44.50 on the NYSE.[170]

Despite Wall Street's fears, the bottom still had not fallen out. Kodak ended the year 2000 with only a 1 percent decline in sales. Its earnings per share actually increased that year to $4.59.[171] Although its R&D expenditures continued to decline to $784 million from $817 million in 1999[172], it still employed 78,400 people, of whom 43,200 were in the United States.[173] Its long-term debt

---

169 *The Wall Street Journal*, Sept. 27, 2000.

170 Ibid.

171 Eastman Kodak Company, Form 10-K annual report for the year ended Dec. 31, 2000, 10.

172 Ibid, 5.

173 Ibid, 6.

increased to $1,166 million from $936 million in 1999.[174] Directly below the line item "Long-term borrowings" on its balance sheet was "Postemployment liabilities" (*pensions*) [emphasis added] in the amount of $2,610 million.[175] Hence, even in the year 2000 its pension obligations were double the amount of its long-term debt.

Of greater importance to Kodak's future was the alteration in the language concerning patents. As of 1999 Kodak still used essentially the same language in its Form 10-K about the materiality of Kodak's patents in the aggregate and the lack of materiality of any single patent or process.[176] Instead, Kodak used completely new language to describe its patents:

> It has been Kodak's general practice to protect its investment in research and development and its freedom to use its inventions by obtaining patents. The ownership of these patents contributes to Kodak's ability to provide leadership products and to generate revenue from licensing. The company holds portfolios of patents in several areas important to its business, including color negative films, processing and papers; digital cameras; network photo fulfillment; and organic light emitting diodes. Each of these areas is important to existent

---

174 Ibid, 33.

175 Ibid, 33.

176 See footnote 66, supra.

and emerging business opportunities that bear directly on the Company's overall business performance. [177]

This statement is the first regulatory evidence of a change in Kodak's strategy seeking to monetize the value of its patents. The year 2000 Form 10-K spoke of its patents as a portfolio—as if they were stock, bonds, or some other assets with monetary value. Within several years, Kodak would come to be increasingly dependent on its ability to monetize its patent portfolio.

The year 2001 was difficult for the nation, its individual citizens, and its corporations. As a result of the terrorist attacks on September 11, 2001, consumers retrenched their spending and the country plunged into recession. For Kodak that year was one of technological and marketing progress, combined with serious continual financial disappointments. The financial disappointments preceded the September 11 terrorist attacks. They were recurrent and of increasing severity.

The reduction in earnings forecasts and layoffs began with first quarter earnings. In January, Kodak said it was comfortable with earnings estimates of $4.50 to $4.90 per share. On April 17, 2001, it withdrew that earnings guidance, announced a pretax restructuring charge of

---

177 Ibid, 6.

$375 to $450 million and announced the elimination of 3,000 to 3,500 worldwide jobs.[178]

The next month at a meeting with investors in New York City, CEO Carp reduced the long-term 8 percent to 12 percent sales growth and 10 percent earnings growth projections made in 1999 by former CEO George Fisher to the range of 5 percent to 7 percent per year.[179] While this was disappointing, in October the news would be worse. On October 24, 2001 Kodak reported a 77 percent decline in third quarter earnings, cut its fourth quarter guidance, and announced new additional layoffs of 3,500 to 4000 workers. Hence Kodak's layoffs planned for 2001 would be between 6,500 and 7,500 workers . As if this were not enough, it also announced a decline in its US market share for film.[180] As the bad news was announced, Kodak stock hit a 15-year low of $28.57 on the NYSE.[181] The stock closed with a loss of $3.46 at $30.71.[182] This price was $10 lower than Kodak's 2000 buyback of 21.6 million of its shares at an average price of $41.[183]

---

178 See "Kodak Edges Forecasts, but Plans Layoffs, Retracts 2001 Guidance," *The Wall Street Journal*, April 18, 2001, B4.

179 See "Kodak Scales Back Growth Projections," *The Wall Street Journal*, May 3, 2001.

180 See "Kodak Net Plummets 77% on Weak Sales," *The Wall Street Journal*, Oct. 25, 2001.

181 "Kodak Profits to Fall, to Cut More Jobs," Reuters, Oct. 24, 2001, 12:09 p.m. Eastern Time.

182 See "Kodak Net Plummets 77% on Weak Sales," *The Wall Street Journal*, Oct. 25, 2001.

183 See *RealMoney.com*, "LSI Logic Is Hard to Fathom," Oct. 30, 2001.

On the technological front 2001 was for Kodak a year of digital progress. Kodak invented its EasyShare system to make digital cameras easier to interface with personal computers. After several conflicts with Microsoft over compatibility with its Windows XP operating system,[184] Kodak gained market share in digital cameras against Sony Corporation.[185]

Despite gaining market share in digital cameras, Kodak was faced with two problems. First, the average selling price for digital cameras was declining by almost $50 per year. Second, Kodak still resisted selling its own inkjet printer, instead relying of 24,000 printing kiosks in retail stores.[186] The annual declines in average selling prices of digital cameras caused a profitability problem for Kodak. How could it ever hope to make profits on digital cameras if they were forever declining in price? The failure to make or market a digital inkjet printer exposed the company to loss of market share for prints to the manufacturers of printers, such as Hewlett-Packard.

In 2001 Kodak's sales declined 5 percent to $13,234 million, but earnings per share declined 94 percent to $ .26 from $4.59 the year before.[187] Its R&D continued

---

184 See "*Shutter Bug*—New Digital Camera Deals Kodak a Lesson in Microsoft's Ways," *The Wall Street Journal,* July 1, 2001.

185 "Kodak Advances In Market Share of Digital Cameras," *The Wall Street Journal,* Dec. 21, 2001.

186 "Kodak Is the Picture of Digital Success," *Business Week,* Jan. 14, 2002, 39.

187 Eastman Kodak Company, Form 10-K annual report for the year ended Dec. 31, 2001, 15.

to decline to $779 million from $784 million the year before.[188] Its worldwide employment declined from 78,400 in 2000 to 75,100 in 2001. Its US employment declined from 43,200 in 2000 to 42,000 in 2001.[189] Its long-term debt increased from $1,166 million in 2000 to $1,666 million in 2001. Its postemployment liabilities increased from $2,610 million in 2000 to $2,728 million in 2001.[190]

In its year 2000 Form 10-K, Kodak had changed its language describing its use of patents "to generate revenue from licensing."[191] The company continued similar language in its 2001 Form 10-K, with the following additional sentences:

> The company is beginning *to leverage its patent portfolio, which has started to generate royalty income. Amounts to date have not been significant, but could be material in the future.* [emphasis added][192]

Kodak elaborated on its new patent strategy under the "RISK FACTORS" section of its 2001 Form 10- K:

---

188 Ibid, 7.

189 Ibid, 8.

190 Ibid, 60.

191 See footnote 177, supra.

192 Ibid, 8.

Kodak's ability to *implement its intellectual property licensing strategies* could also affect the Company 's *revenues and earnings.* Kodak has invested millions of dollars in technologies and needs to protect its intellectual property. The establishment and enforcement of licensing agreements provides a *revenue stream* that protects Kodak's ability to further innovate and help the marketplace grow. Kodak's failure to properly manage the development of its intellectual property could adversely affect the future of these patents and the market opportunities that could result from the use of this property. Kodak's failure to manage the costs associated with the *pursuit of these licenses could adversely affect the profitability of these operations.* [emphasis added][193]

Without expressly defining its "intellectual property licensing strategies," Kodak made clear its intention to seek revenue from "licensing agreements" to provide a "revenue stream." Kodak's business model changed from only sales and manufacturing of products to monetizing patents by licensing agreements. Once again, did Kodak ever ask if this is something that George Eastman would have done? Kodak entered a nontraditional business with limited experience in the field. By 2012 the consequences of this strategy change would be fatal.

---

193 Ibid, 49.

Moreover, this new strategy was outside the scope of its business described in Part I, ITEM 1 of its 2001 Form 10-K: *primarily* developing, manufacturing and marketing of imaging products.[194] In defense of Kodak, it can be argued that in 2001 the company's business was *primarily* sales of imaging products, and that in that year patent licensing royalties had not been *significant*. Hence, Kodak appeared to be in technical compliance with disclosure requirements in its 2001 Form 10-K.

Was it proper to engage in such collateral activities without either a modification of Kodak's Certificate of Doing Business or adding "patent licensing" to a description of its basic business in the very first item on its annual Form 10-K? Did the board of directors ever vote to authorize this new collateral strategy?

During the time period when this change of strategy occurred, there was considerable turmoil in Kodak's executive suite. In a twelve-month period, Kodak lost no fewer than seven top executives. Gone were the president of the health imaging division, the senior VP of human resources, the president of the professional imaging division, the senior VP of digital business development, the regional president of consumer imaging, the chief quality officer, and the president and chief operating officer, Patricia F. Russo. She suddenly

---

194 Ibid, p., 2.

resigned after only nine months on the job.[195] She left to become CEO of telecommunications company Lucent Technologies.

In 2001 Daniel Carp was (1) chairman of the board and (2) chief executive officer.[196] As a result of Russo's departure, in 2002 Daniel Carp was (1) chairman of the board, (2) chief executive officer, (3) president, and (4) chief operating officer.[197] This increased the work burden on Daniel Carp, but also raised corporate governance issues concerning the concentration of so much power in one corporate officer.

While Kodak continued to gain market share in digital cameras, it also continued to be hurt by the decline in average selling prices. The EasyShare system increased its US market share for digital cameras from number three in the year 2000 to number two in 2001. Even though sales volume of digital cameras grew 35 percent in 2001, net sales actually decreased 3 percent.[198] Kodak's 10-K failed to disclose the dollar amounts of sales and earnings attributable to digital cameras.

In order to cut costs, Kodak in 2002 decided to move a large portion of its manufacturing of one-time-use

---

195 See "President Resigns from Kodak," Rochester *Democrat and Chronicle*, Jan. 8, 2002, 1A.

196 Eastman Kodak Company, Form 10-K annual report for the year ended Dec. 31, 2001, 10.

197 Eastman Kodak Company, Form 10-K annual report for the year ended Dec. 31, 2002, 13.

198 Ibid, 37.

cameras to China.[199] This confirmed previous fears of Kodak Park Rochester employees that their jobs would be lost to cheaper workers in China.

In 2002 Kodak also moved belatedly to rectify its lack of inkjet printers. In January, 2002, it acquired ENCAD, Inc., which provided printers, inks, and software to the commercial printing industry.[200] Kodak continued neither to market nor to sell an amateur inkjet printer.

Kodak's restructurings were becoming annual Christmas time events. It announced a fourth quarter restructuring relating to its relocation of one-time-use camera production to China. It took a restructuring charge of $116 million for the severance of 1,150 employees.[201] As a result of these constant restructurings, Kodak's financial statements became increasingly difficult to compare to each other, to analyze, and to understand.

In 2002 Kodak's sales declined 3 percent to $12,835 million, its earnings per share increased 915 percent to $2.64 from $.26 the year before.[202] Its R&D continued to decline to $762 million from $779 million the year before.[203] Its worldwide employment declined

---

199 Ibid, 4.

200 Ibid, 7.

201 Ibid, "Restructuring Costs and Other," 45.

202 Ibid, 42.

203 Ibid, 10.

to 70,000[204] from 75,100 in 2001. Its US employment declined to 39,000[205] from 42,000 in 2001. Its long-term debt decreased to $1,164 million[206] from $1,666 in 2001. However, its postretirement liabilities increased from $2,728 million in 2001 to $3,412 million in 2002.[207] Of greater immediate concern to shareholders was the reduction in the annual cash dividend per share from $2.21 per share in 2001 to $1.80 per share in 2002.[208] As many shareholders lived in the Rochester area, the reduction in the dividend hurt the local economy. Also, the dividend reduction raised a serious warning flag for all long-term investors in Eastman Kodak Company common stock. If Kodak could not afford to maintain its dividend, then it was likely the share price would fall. It also raised the possibility of further dividend cuts in the future. But in 2002, no one could reasonably foresee that the dividend would be entirely eliminated, that is, go to zero. Things would not improve the next year; they would get much worse.

The year 2003 was the year Kodak started to fall apart. Kodak could not stop restructuring. On January 22, 2003, it announced it intended to terminate 1,800 to 2,200 more employees. It expected to incur charges

---

204 Ibid, 11.
205 Ibid., 11.
206 Ibid, 80.
207 Ibid, 80.
208 Ibid, 79.

in the range of $75 million to $100 million for these lay-offs.[209] The problem was that cost-cutting could not prevent the decline in profitability caused by the growth of digital photography at the expense of film. It was estimated that Wal-Mart accounted for about 25 percent to 30 percent of the market for domestic photofinishing. Wal-Mart had a contract with Fuji for photofinishing supplies and paper.[210] Lack of demand for color photofinishing paper, and decline in demand for roll film, meant that Kodak was in a losing race to cut costs as the market for digital cameras exploded.

On January 22, 2003 Kodak forecast annual earnings in the range of $2.35 to $2.95 per share. The stock closed down $4.41 to $33.18 on the NYSE. [211] What disturbed investors was Kodak's downbeat forecast for the future of film. Thirteen years earlier it had forecast that by 2010, 30 percent of all photographs would be through electronic imaging.[212] Conversely, this meant that in 2010, 70 percent of all photographs would be through traditional film and chemicals. In 2003, Kodak seemed to abandon that forecast. Kodak said that in 2002, digital imaging reduced film consumption by 3 percent, and that it expected that in 2003 digital imaging would reduce film consumption by 4 percent to 5 percent and continue to grow thereaf-

209 Ibid, 46.

210 *New York Times,* "Market Insight," Jan. 26, 2003.

211 Rochester *Democrat and Chronicle,* Jan. 23, 2003.

212 See footnote 8, supra.

ter.[213] Daniel Carp stated that after 2006, "we'll see a *slow decay* of film in the United States"[214] [emphasis added].

He was more optimistic about the international markets, where film would continue to remain: "viable...for a longer period." [215]

He also indicated that single-use cameras will stay around "forever."[216]

There is evidence that Kodak's hostility to computer inkjet printers came directly from the top. In an article in *Business Week,* the CEO recounted how he almost missed the third quarter of the Super Bowl because he was using his computer printer. He called the experience "miserable."[217] Kodak intended to introduce a $199 computer printer in May, 2003. Meanwhile, it would rely on its 23,000 photo kiosks, which some consumers found intimidating.[218] Prior to the digital era, consumers would take their roll film to a local minilab to be processed into prints. As the digital era arrived, consumers would take their memory cards to a local minilab to be processed into prints. By 2003 Fuji had 5,000 minilabs in place and

---

213 Rochester *Democrat and Chronicle,* Jan. 23, 2003.

214 Ibid.

215 Ibid.

216 Ibid.

217 *Business Week,* Mar. 24, 2003, 80.

218 Ibid, 81.

had 60 percent of the US minilab market.[219] Compared to its Japanese competitor, Kodak seemed lethargic, less nimble, and unable to cope effectively with changes in the photography market.

Kodak's first quarter earnings in 2003 were disastrous. Its net income fell to only $12 million or $.04 per share from $39 million or $.13 per share in 2002.[220] In the first quarter of 2003, Kodak's film sales declined 24 percent in the United States, and its market share of consumer digital cameras declined from the fourth quarter of 2002.[221]

Kodak's second quarter earnings in 2003 declined 60 percent to $.39 from $.97 in 2002. Kodak announced job cuts of 4,500 to 6,000 worldwide and between 2,000 to 3,000 in Rochester.[222] Kodak was still Rochester's largest employer with about 21,600 local employees.[223] CEO Daniel Carp stated, "I think we're at the point where we have to get on with reality: The consumer traditional business is going to begin *a slow decline though it's not going to fall off a cliff"*[224] [emphasis added].

---

219 Ibid, 80.

220 See "Kodak Profit Falls as Film Demand Fades," *Reuters*, April 23, 2003, 8:49 a.m. ET.

221 See "Photography—A New Picture—*For Photo-film Makers, Digital Advances Offer an Opportunity – and a Threat*," The Wall Street Journal, May 19, 2003, R17.

222 Rochester *Democrat and Chronicle*, July 24, 2003, 8A.

223 Ibid.

224 Ibid, 1A.

In the midst of Kodak's 2003 earnings problems, it reorganized its management, emphasizing leaders with digital or computer experience. Its new president, Antonio Perez, and the new head of its commercial digital-printing unit both came from Hewlett-Packard. The head of its photography unit came from Lexmark International.[225] As a result of the reorganization, except for the CEO himself, most of the top management came from outside Kodak.[226]

While Kodak was playing "musical chairs" with its top management, its finances continued to deteriorate. As of September 21, 2003, its corporate debt was only one notch above junk rating by Moody's Investors Service.[227] The shocker would come on September 25, 2003. On that day, Kodak did the once unthinkable: it reduced its semiannual dividend by 72 percent from $.90 per share to $.25 per share. Its share price declined 18 percent or $4.84 on the NYSE to close at $22.15. Standard & Poor's downgraded Kodak's debt to one notch above speculative.[228]

Management's rationale for the dividend cut was to preserve cash to invest in new digital products, including

---

225 See "Kodak Answers Digital's Siren," *The Wall Street Journal*, Aug. 22, 2003, B4.

226 See "Kodak Shifts Focus From Film, Betting Future On Digital Lines," *The Wall Street Journal*, Sept. 21, 2003.

227 Ibid.

228 *The Wall Street Journal*, Sept. 26, 2003, B6.

inkjet printers. Kodak had ignored this market for years. Its hometown rival, Xerox, had tried and failed to enter this market. Analysts were skeptical that Kodak could succeed where Xerox had failed.[229] Other analysts questioned whether Kodak had the manufacturing competence to achieve worthwhile returns on inkjet printers. It was argued that instead of wasting money to buy its own stock when it was over $70 per share, Kodak should have spent the money making inkjet printers years ago.[230]

Local residents, who had previously been ridiculed as shortsighted, narrow-minded, and paranoid when they criticized Kodak's diminishing commitment to Rochester, now could say, "I told you so." The Chinese factories would indeed be used to replace Rochester jobs. The previous year Kodak had relocated its one-time-use camera production to China.[231] This had cost $116 million and had resulted in the severance of 1,150 employees. In July, 2003 it announced it was moving the packaging portion of film manufacturing to Mexico and China, resulting in 800 more local layoffs.[232] Some local residents, who depended on the income from Kodak's dividend, were shocked. Others refused to diversify and still held their shares.[233]

---

229 Rochester *Democrat and Chronicle*, Sept. 26, 2003, 6A.

230 See "Ahead of the Tape," *The Wall Street Journal*, Sept. 26, 2003.

231 See footnote 201, supra.

232 Rochester *Democrat and Chronicle*, Sept. 26, 2003, 6A.

233 See "Loyal Shareholders' Faith Shaken," Rochester *Democrat and Chronicle*, Sept. 26, 2003, 6A.

Kodak's abrupt change in strategy antagonized not only individual shareholders. Institutional shareholders were particularly annoyed when they learned that the dividend had been slashed 72 percent so that Kodak could use $3 billion to buy new businesses.[234] One institutional activist shareholder organized a meeting in New York City to persuade Kodak to alter its decision. When questioned about the new strategy, a Kodak spokesman said: "The one we announced is one we think offers investors the best opportunity for growth and to maximize value of their investments."[235]

While some institutional investors sold their shares, others bought. Kodak's largest shareholder, Legg Mason Funds, increased its holdings to 28.7 million shares.[236] Among the new shareholders was financier Carl Icahn.[237]

Kodak started to implement its new strategy by buying the digital printing business of Israeli company Scitex Corp. for $250 million. The company made high-speed digital inkjet printers. Kodak had previously sold the same digital printing company to Scitex in 1993 for $70 million.[238] Had Kodak simply done nothing—not sold the

234 See "Kodak Strategy May Set off Battle," Rochester *Democrat and Chronicle*, Oct. 11, 2003.

235 See "Investors Seek to Rewind Kodak," *The Wall Street Journal*, Oct. 21, 2003, C1.

236 See "Strategies—Not Exactly a Kodak Moment," *Business Week*, Nov. 24, 2003, 44.

237 "Billionaire Icahn Hovers over Kodak," Rochester *Democrat and Chronicle*, Nov. 4, 2003,1A.

238 *The Wall Street Journal*, Nov. 26, 2003.

company in 1993—it would have saved $180 million. Shortly thereafter, Standard & Poor's revised Kodak's credit rating to negative, putting its bonds near junk status.[239] In 2003, Kodak had purchased the following companies:

1. *Applied Science Fiction for $32 million.*
2. *MiraMedica Inc. for an undisclosed price.*
3. *LaserPacific for $30.5 million.*
4. *Practice Works for $486 million.*
5. *Algotec Systems for $42.5 million.*
6. *Scitex Digital Printing for $250 million.[240]*
    Total spent: at least $841 million.

Once again no one seems to have asked, Is this something George Eastman would have done? Would George Eastman have cut the dividend by 72 percent? Would George Eastman have used the proceeds to go on a buying spree of smaller companies? Would George Eastman have sold something for $70 million and bought it back ten years later for $250 million? In view of Kodak's bankruptcy, the answers are probably a resounding "No."

In 2003 Kodak's sales increased 4 percent to $13,317 million.[241]Its earnings per share decreased to $.92 from $2.64 the year before.[242] While its R&D actually increased by $19 million to $781 million from $762 million the year

239 "S&P Raps Kodak Buying Spree," Rochester *Democrat and Chronicle*, Nov. 29, 2003.

240 Ibid, 2A.

241 Eastman Kodak Company, Form 10-K annual report for the year ended Dec. 31, 2003, 27.

242 Ibid, 41.

before, its R&D expenditures on photography continued to decline. For example, in 2000 it spent $575 million on Photography R&D, in 2001 it spent $542 million, and in 2002 it spent $513 million.[243] In 2003, Kodak spent $481 million on photography.[244] The 10-K Forms did not contain a breakdown or apportionment between film and digital photography R&D. However, the steady decline in R&D year after year calls into question Kodak's digital strategy, which would probably require increasing digital R&D expenditures for competitive purposes.

In 2003, Kodak's worldwide employment declined to 63,900 people[245] from 70,000 in 2002. In 2003, its US employment declined to 35,400 people[246] from 39,000 in 2002.

Kodak's balance sheet in 2003 continued to deteriorate. While its postretirement liabilities declined slightly to $3,344 million in 2003 from $3,412 million in 2002,[247] its long-term debt more than doubled to $2,302 million from $1,164 in 2002.[248] At least $841 million of the increase in long-term debt was probably the result of its acquisitions of six companies in 2003. As of December

---

243 Eastman Kodak Company, Form 10-K annual report for the year ended Dec. 31, 2002, 10.

244 Eastman Kodak Company, Form 10-K annual report for the year ended Dec. 31, 2003, 13.

245 Ibid, 13.

246 Ibid, 13.

247 Ibid, 94.

248 Ibid, 94.

31, 2003, all three major ratings services (Moody's, S & P, and Fitch) had a negative outlook for Kodak.[249]

Kodak's fourth quarter 2003 earnings were announced at 3:00 a.m. on January 22, 2004.[250] The only positive news was the increase in sales of digital products. Sales of EasyShare digital cameras increased 87 percent, and sales of digital X-ray products increased 26 percent. However, earnings per share declined to only $.07 from $.39 in the fourth quarter of 2002.[251]To deal with the deterioration in its finances, Kodak announced a drastic restructuring. Kodak planned to cut its work force by 12,000 to 15,000 jobs by 2006, and incur writeoffs of $1.3 billion to $1.7 billion. Kodak also planned to downsize its factories by almost one-third.[252] One week earlier, Kodak also announced it was ending its Advanced Photo System.[253] The introduction of the APS had been announced to sipping champagne and dancing years earlier at the George Eastman House. The life of this product, once touted by Kodak as "the most significant consumer product introduction in 30 years,"[254] was only eight years.

---

249 Ibid, 71.

250 Rochester *Democrat and Chronicle*, Jan. 22, 2004.

251 Ibid, 6A.

252 See "Kodak to Cut Staff up to 21%, Amid Digital Push," *The Wall Street Journal*, Jan. 22, 2004

253 Ibid.

254 See footnote 71, supra.

As of December 31, 2003, Kodak was still Rochester's largest employer, with 20,600 local employees.[255] With the announcement of the coming layoffs, it was certain that Kodak would lose this position. To the mayor of Rochester the announcement felt like "an assault."[256]

While the massive layoffs were bad news for Rochester, Wall Street had a different opinion. On the day of the announcement, Kodak's shares climbed $3.49 to close at $30.95 on the NYSE.[257]

Although Kodak's financial engineering had been interpreted by the stock market as a success, Kodak's efforts to dominate digital photography would fail, largely due to the cell phone camera. As early as December 22, 2003, the financial press had publicized this "hot" new market.[258] Where was Kodak? It seemed to ignore the growing market for cameras in cell phones. The new camera phones were easy to use and could be carried in a pocket anywhere. They enabled consumers to view and e-mail their photos instantly. While Kodak was laying off tens of thousands of loyal workers, cutting its dividend, and investing in small companies, it was blind to

---

255 Rochester *Democrat and Chronicle*, Jan. 22, 2004, 1A.

256 See "Tech Blessing Becomes Rochester's Curse," *The Wall Street Journal*, Jan. 23, 2004.

257 See "Kodak Estimates a Broad Range for 2004 Profit," *The Wall Street Journal*, Jan. 24, 2004.

258 See "CELL PHONES—America Zooms in on Camera Phones, " *Business Week*, Dec. 22, 2003, 44.

the fastest growing digital market of all: cell phone cameras. It was estimated that cell phone cameras would grow from almost nothing in 2002 to 5 million units in 2003.[259] Kodak's blindness was perplexing, because CEO Carp had been a protégé of former CEO Fisher, who had come to Kodak from Motorola. As camera phones began to eat into the lower end of the digital camera market, Kodak responded by enabling its photo kiosks to print camera phone photos.[260]

One can speculate as to why Kodak was blind to this technological revolution. Perhaps it was the old mentality that "We *are* the market." Perhaps Kodak thought it could rely on licensing revenue to produce an income stream from royalties on sales of cell phones by third parties. Perhaps Kodak was too involved in financial restructuring to realize what was happening in the cell phone market. Had Kodak entered that market in 2003, it might have dominated it. But there was no Kodak cell phone in 2003. Tragically, it let other companies do what Kodak could have, and should have, done. It surrendered an enormous new market without even a fight.

In his meeting with investors and analysts in New York City on January 22, 2004, CEO Carp stated, "It would be a crime to be timid."[261]

---

259 Ibid.

260 See "The Camera Phone Revolution," *Business Week,* April 12, 2004, 52.

261 Rochester *Democrat and Chronicle,* Jan. 23, 2004, 8A.

That would have been the perfect time to introduce an EasyShare cell phone. Instead, it was indicated that about 5,000 Rochester employees would be laid off and that profits would increase 30 percent and sales would increase 25 percent by the end of 2006.[262] Someone in the audience should have asked, "Then what?"

Kodak's plans to downsize its real estate holdings began in Rochester. Twenty-four buildings were scheduled for demolition at Kodak Park in 2004.[263] Opened by George Eastman in 1890, Kodak Park, by 2004, contained almost 1300 acres and 151 buildings.[264] The 2004 demolitions would still leave more than 100 buildings, along with possible chemical contamination and environmental pollution.[265]

Meanwhile, Chief Operating Officer Perez had made a thorough examination of Kodak's 20,000 patents. In an interview with a business magazine, he indicated that Kodak had found a breakthrough technology for its inkjet printers. In particular he was quoted as saying, "The intellectual property and know-how is unbelievable in the company...There is no excuse not to succeed."[266]

262 Ibid.

263 Rochester *Democrat and Chronicle,* April 18, 2004, 1A.

264 Ibid, 10A.

265 Ibid, 10A, "Film Manufacturing's Leftover Pollution Prompts Concerns."

266 *Business Week,* May 10, 2004, 96.

In January, 2004 Kodak had predicted that film sales would decline 10 percent to 12 percent. However, a mid-year survey indicated that the decline was 16 percent.[267] In another meeting with investors in New York City on September 22, 2004, Kodak argued that the increase in its digital business would compensate for the decline in film. It said sales of its digital products would grow 36 percent per year from 2003 to 2007.[268]

A milestone in Kodak's transformation from film to digital occurred on November 18, 2004. On that day Kodak ended production of its most successful product: the slide projector.[269] The Carousel projector had been an ingenious product. Round slide trays had used gravity to feed individual 35mm slides into a projector where they could be enlarged in darkened rooms onto silver screens.

While employees continued to be cut right and left at Kodak Park, the situation was entirely the opposite at Kodak's factories in China. There employees were paid $5.75 per day. Toward the end of 2004, almost 95 percent of Kodak's cameras were made there.[270]

No attempt thus far has been made to analyze Kodak's financials for 2004. As early as February 9, 2004, Kodak's

---

267 *The Wall Street Journal*, Sept. 4, 2004, "Fall of Film Sales Exceeds Forecast by Kodak."

268 See "Kodak Raises Forecast for Digital Sales," *The Wall Street Journal*, Sept. 23, 2004.

269 Rochester *Democrat and Chronicle*, Nov. 19, 2004, 1A.

270 *Forbes*, Nov. 15, 2004, 190.

accounting had been publicly questioned.[271] What Kodak did not need were accounting problems. Sure enough, on March 16, 2005, Kodak announced it would restate its results for 2003 and 2004, which would lower earnings because of accounting errors. It applied for an extension of time to report its March 31, 2005, results. It said it had a "material weakness" in accounting for retirement benefits and income taxes.[272] If long-term investors had ever needed a red flag saying, "Sell," this had to be it. How could Kodak transform itself from film to digital if it couldn't accurately count its own numbers?

On April 6, 2005, Kodak issued a press release describing "inadvertent accounting errors" and indicating that its 2004 Annual Report Form 10-K was finally filed with the US Securities and Exchange Commission.[273]

There were two material differences between the 2003 Form 10-K and the 2004 Form 10-K. First, the photography segment was renamed Digital & Film Imaging Systems (D&FIS). Second, "ITEM 3. LEGAL PROCEEDINGS" disclosed patent litigation against Sony Corporation and Sun Microsystems. While the Sony lawsuit was still pending, the Sun lawsuit resulted in an October 1, 2004, jury verdict in Kodak's favor that Sun had infringed on Kodak's patents.

---

271 See "Kodak's Fuzzy Numbers—The Company Has Taken 'One-time' Charges Every Year for the Past 12," *Business Week*, February 9, 2004, 77.

272 See "Kodak to Restate Results for '03, '04," *The Wall Street Journal*, March 17, 2005.

273 "Business Wire," April 06, 2005, 08:55 a.m., Eastern Daylight Time.

The case was settled on October 12, 2004, and Sun paid Kodak $92 million in cash.[274] Kodak had successfully monetized some intellectual property in its patent portfolio.

In 2004, Kodak's sales increased 5 percent to $13,517 million.[275] Its earnings per share increased to $1.97 from $.88 the year before.[276] While its total R&D increased to $854 million from $776 million the year before, its D&FIS expenditures decreased to $368 million from a restated $481 million the year before. There was no breakdown or apportionment between film and digital R&D.[277]

In 2004, Kodak's worldwide employment declined to 54,800[278] from 63,900 in 2003. In 2004 its US employment declined to 29,200[279] from 35,400 people in 2003.

In 2004, its long-term debt decreased to $1,852 million from $2,302 million in 2003. Its pension and other postretirement liabilities decreased to $3,338 million from $3,374 million in 2003.[280]

Its debt ratings from Moody's and S&P did not change from 2003 to 2004. It no longer retained Fitch to rate

---

274 Eastman Kodak Company, Form 10-K annual report for the year ended Dec. 31, 2004, 11.

275 Ibid, 25.

276 Ibid, 39.

277 Ibid, 10.

278 Ibid, 11.

279 Ibid, 11.

280 Ibid, 81.

its debt. On February 1, 2005, Fitch downgraded Kodak's ratings on its long-term debt and withdrew its ratings on Kodak's short-term debt.[281]

Despite its embarrassing accounting problems, Kodak made enormous progress in market share for digital cameras. When the figures were calculated, Kodak had the number one position in US share of digital cameras in 2004. Kodak led with 22 percent of the market, ahead of Sony with 19 percent, and Canon with 15 percent. Hewlett-Packard had only 8 percent.[282] Kodak's business model of designing products and software in the United States, and outsourcing production to Asia, was compared in the financial press to Apple's iPod.

At this critical time, when Kodak had digital victory within its grasp, Kodak's fifty-seven year old CEO Carp announced that he would leave his CEO post on June 1, 2005, and that he would retire as chairman of the board on December 31, 2005. At the time of the announcement, Kodak held the number-one market position in both digital cameras and consumer printers.[283] While Kodak's stock price rose $1.13 to $26.58 after the announcement, during his tenure as CEO it had declined from $66.25—a drop of almost $40.00 per share.[284]

---

281 Ibid, 63.

282 See "Kodak Leads US in Digital Cameras," *The Wall Street Journal*, February 3, 2005.

283 See "Kodak's Carp to Relinquish Top Jobs," *The Wall Street Journal*, May 12, 2005.

284 Rochester *Democrat and Chronicle*, May 12, 2005. 7A.

7 - Two-Year Deadline
(2005–2007)

The CEO change from Carp to Perez was announced at Kodak's annual meeting on May 11, 2005. In his address to shareholders the new CEO stated: "Our time to act is short...but the next two years are critical. We will have to accelerate the pace of our move into digital."[285]

The two-year deadline for completion of the digital transformation was reiterated in Kodak's 2005 annual report filed with the Securities and Exchange Commission. The first item listed under "Risk Factors" was "If we do not effectively execute our digital transformation, this could adversely affect our operations, revenue and ability to compete."[286]

The first three sentences in the paragraph below this Risk Factor stated:

The company continues with its transformation from a traditional products and services company

---

285 Rochester *Democrat and Chronicle*, May 12, 2005, 6A.

286 Eastman Kodak Company, Form 10-K annual report for the year ended Dec. 31, 2005, 12.

to a digital products and services company. This transformation includes an aggressive restructuring program to reduce its traditional infrastructure to cost-effectively manage the declining traditional business and to reduce its general and administrative costs to the level necessary to compete profitably in the digital markets. The company expects these actions *to be largely completed by mid 2007*.[287] [emphasis added]

The new CEO seemed to be the perfect leader to finish Kodak's digital transformation. He had built Hewlett-Packard's digital printer business into a $10 billion division.[288] Even more important, the HP business model was somewhat similar to Kodak's film business model. HP's printer cartridges were to digital printers what Kodak's film was to cameras. HP's printer cartridges and Kodak's film drove the bottom line like a shaving company that profited from sales of blades, not shavers.

The issue was whether Kodak was then too much of a basket case for him, or anyone else, to save. By the end of 2004, Kodak had the number one market share in the United States for digital cameras.[289] But its traditional film business was in a rapidly accelerating decline.

---

287 Ibid, 12.

288 *Business Week*, May 23, 2005, 42.

289 Eastman Kodak Company, Form 10-K annual report for the year ended Dec. 31, 2005, 48.

In 2004, film sales declined 18 percent, and in 2005, it estimated that film sales would decline 30 percent.[290] Sales of black-and-white photographic printing paper had been declining about 25 percent per year. On June 15, 2005, Kodak announced it would no longer make the black-and-white paper.[291]

In approximately one month after becoming the new CEO, Antonio Perez had his first trial by fire. On July 20, 2005, Kodak reported its financial results for the second quarter. Kodak had a loss of $.51 per share compared to earnings of $.46 per share the year earlier. There were two ominous facts included in the dismal results. First, CEO Perez said Kodak would stop making profit forecasts. This statement suggested that Kodak had lost control of its business. Second, Kodak's Chinese strategy fell apart. Although the company continued to make digital cameras in China, it decided to partially write off its film manufacturing operations there. [292] This had been Kodak's first new photographic film plant in almost thirty years. Kodak had expected the plant to make 100 million rolls of photographic film each year.[293] Now Kodak suddenly discovered that the decline in film sales had spread

---

290 See "Kodak Reports 2004 Results; Restates 2003," *The Wall Street Journal,* April 7, 2005.

291 See "Kodak Dropping Black-and-White Photo Paper," Rochester *Democrat and Chronicle,* June 16, 2005.

292 See "Kodak Posts Loss, Sets More Job Cuts as Film Sales Sink," *The Wall Street Journal,* July 21, 2005.

293 See footnote 141, supra.

to China. Kodak would have to restructure its Chinese film manufacturing. Apparently, management did not see this coming. In 2003 Kodak invested $100 million in China Lucky Film Corp., part of which it had to write down.[294]

Rochester would again pay the price for Kodak's losses. Kodak announced it would cut 10,000 more jobs and get rid of $2 billion in manufacturing assets.[295]

The turmoil in Kodak's operations was accompanied by simultaneous collateral problems. On August 9, 2005, Kodak disclosed that the Securities and Exchange Commission was conducting an informal investigation into the restatement of Kodak's 2003 and 2004 earnings.[296] Then an assessment review board of a Rochester suburb doubled Kodak's property assessment, which could cost Kodak more than $1.5 million in additional property taxes.[297]

In a presentation to investors and stock analysts the next month, CEO Perez did not make any sales or earnings forecasts for 2005 or 2006. He admitted that digital profits would be less than the company had earlier forecast in 2005, but predicted that by 2008, 80 percent

---

294 See footnote 292, supra.

295 Rochester *Democrat and Chronicle*, July 21, 2005, 1A.

296 Rochester *Democrat and Chronicle*, Aug. 10, 2005, 10D.

297 See "Kodak Assessment Doubled," Rochester *Democrat and Chronicle*, Aug. 14, 2005, 1B.

of Kodak's revenues would be digital. The chief financial officer said Kodak didn't need to eliminate its dividend.[298]

Kodak continued to accumulate debt in order to fund its acquisitions of digital companies. On June 15, 2005, it acquired Creo, Inc. for the sum of $967 million. It was a supplier to the commercial printing industry.[299]

On October 19, 2005, Kodak announced its third quarter results. Its digital revenues grew 47 percent to $1.9 billion. Its digital earnings increased to $10 million from $6 million in 2004. However, Kodak reported a net loss for the quarter of $1.029 billion or -$3.58 per share. Its stock declined to $22.06 on the NYSE.[300]

This was too much for the rating agencies to tolerate. Between April 29, 2005, and January 31, 2006, Moody's downgraded its ratings on Kodak debt four times. Standard & Poor's downgraded its ratings on Kodak's debt five times in 2005.[301]

In its eagerness to transform itself from film to digital, Kodak had used leverage. Its cash declined from

298 See "Kodak Scales Back Short-Term View but Sees Revival," *The Wall Street Journal*, Sept. 29, 2005.

299 Eastman Kodak Company, Form 10-K annual report for the year ended Dec. 31, 2005, 136.

300 See "Kodak Digital Outpaces Film Sales," Rochester *Democrat and Chronicle*, Oct. 20, 2005, 1A.

301 Eastman Kodak Company, Form 10-K annual report for the year ended Dec. 31, 2005, 66.

$1.26 billion at the end of 2004 to $610 million near the end of 2005, while its debt increased from $1.24 billion to $3.56 billion.[302] When the financial crisis known as the "Great Recession" struck the world economy two years later, the leverage would cause difficulties for Kodak. In defense of Kodak, it can be argued that few others foresaw the coming economic collapse. And when the subprime problem emerged, even the chairman of the Federal Reserve Board said it was "contained." Only $750 million of Kodak's debt came due in 2006, and its $2.7 billion of remaining debt did not come due until 2010.[303] However, by reducing its cash and increasing its debt, Kodak was gambling that there would not be a major decline in the level of economic activity when its debt had to be repaid. It put itself at the mercy of external forces it could not control. Once again, is this something George Eastman would have done?

Kodak's efforts to monetize its patent portfolio of intellectual property failed to produce monetary benefits in 2005. In 2004 it had received $92 million in a settlement with Sun Microsystems.[304] It did not receive any settlement or verdict money in 2005.[305]

---

302 *Barron's*, "Kodak's Moment," Nov. 21, 2005, 27.

303 See "A Tense Kodak Moment," *Business Week*, Oct. 17, 2005, 84.

304 See footnote 274, supra.

305 See Eastman Kodak Company, Form 10-K annual report for the year ended Dec. 31, 2005, 36.

In 2005, Kodak's sales increased 6 percent to $14,268 million.[306] According to its Form 10-K, its earnings per share decreased 344 percent to -$4.73 from $1.94 the year before.[307] According to its Form 10-K, while its R&D increased to $892 million from $836 million the year before, its D&FIS expenditures decreased to $276 million from $365 the year before.[308]

In 2005, Kodak's worldwide employment declined to 51,100[309] from 54,800. In 2005, its US employment declined to 25,500[310] from 29,200 the year before.

According to its Form 10-K, its long-term debt increased to $2,764 million in 2005[311] from $1,852 million the year before. According to its Form 10-K , its pension and other postretirement liabilities increased in 2005 to $3,476 million from $3,338 million the year before.

At the beginning of 2006, Kodak was still the largest manufacturer of roll film, followed by Fuji in second place, and then by Konica Minolta in third place. On January 19, 2006, Konica Minolta announced it would [312]

---

306 Ibid, 34.

307 Ibid, 54.

308 Ibid, 10.

309 Ibid, 11.

310 Ibid, 11.

311 Ibid, 79.

312 See "Konica drops photography," Rochester *Democrat and Chronicle*, Jan. 20, 2006, 10D.

stop making film, photographic paper, film cameras, and digital cameras. Minolta had revolutionized the 35mm camera market by marketing the first film camera with an autofocus system.

Kodak's response in 2006 was not to abandon the film market, but to separate it from its digital units for financial reporting purposes. In 2005, its consumer imaging unit was named Digital & Film Imaging Systems (D&FIS). As of January 1, 2006, D&FIS was split into two distinct units: (1) Consumer Digital Imaging Group Segment and (2) Film and Photofinishing Systems Group Segment. The remaining other business segments in 2006 were (3) Health Group Segment, (4) Graphic Communications Group Segment, and (5) All other.[313]

The separation of the photography units into new digital and old film segments would for the first time permit full annual disclosure of sales, earnings, and profitability of Kodak's digital business. It would also make the sale or divestiture of any segment more transparent.

Rather than selling or spinning off its film unit, Kodak instead announced on May 4, 2006, that it had retained Goldman, Sachs & Co. to explore changes for the Health Group Segment.[314]

---

313 Eastman Kodak Company, Form 10-K annual report for the year ended Dec. 31, 2005, 4.

314 See "Kodak Might Sell Unit," Rochester *Democrat and Chronicle*, May 4, 2006, 1A.

The noise associated with the announcement that Kodak might sell its Health Group segment distracted some investors from the operating results for the first quarter, which were released on the same day. The results were quite poor. For the first quarter of 2006, Kodak lost $298 million or -$1.04 per share. Sales of its digital products segment declined 10 percent to $498 million. The digital products segment did not earn money in the first quarter of 2006. It lost $94 million before income taxes.[315]

Kodak continued to lose money in the second quarter of 2006. It lost $282 million or -$.98 per share, compared with a loss of $155 million or -$.54 the year before. Its digital camera segment again showed a loss. Its stock declined $3.05 on the NYSE to close at $19.20.[316] It announced 2,000 more layoffs, and said it would outsource manufacturing of its Kodak- branded digital cameras to Flextronics International,[317] a company headquartered in Singapore. The Kodak press release also disclosed that Flextronics would handle distribution of the Kodak digital cameras, as well as certain design and development functions. It stated that Kodak would retain its intellectual property.[318]

---

315 See "Digital Photography Shows a Loss," Rochester *Democrat and Chronicle,* May 5, 2006, 7A.

316 See "Kodak's Loss Widens as Revenue Declines 8.8%," *The Wall Street Journal,* Aug. 2, 2006, B10.

317 Ibid.

318 See Press Release, Aug. 1, 2006, 7:02 a.m. ET.

Kodak had set a 2006 target of $350–$450 million in digital earnings. For the first half of 2006, its digital operations showed a $30 million loss. Investment analysts were becoming increasingly skeptical of Kodak's ability to profit from its digital photography products.[319] Kodak's market share of digital cameras declined to third place at only 15 percent, behind leaders Canon and Sony.[320]

Kodak's credit quality continued to deteriorate. On May 5, 2006, Moody's put Kodak on review for a possible downgrade. On August 2, 2006 Standard & Poor's made a similar move.[321]

In 2006, for the first time, Kodak's digital revenues exceeded its traditional revenues.[322]However, its sales actually declined from $14,268 million in 2005 to $13,274 million in 2006.[323] A detailed analysis of 2006 indicates that sales of Kodak's digital products actually declined from $3,215 million in 2005 to $2,920 million in 2006. Thus, although Kodak's digital sales in 2006 exceeded its traditional sales, the digital products group was not growing—it was shrinking.

---

319 See *Barron's*, "For Ailing Kodak, the Picture Dims," Aug. 7, 2006, 14.

320 *The Value Line Investment Survey*, Sept. 1, 2006, 134.

321 Eastman Kodak Company, Form 10-K annual report for the year ended Dec. 31, 2006, 64.

322 Ibid, 4.

323 Ibid, 76.

Even Kodak's R&D on digital products was shrinking in 2006. While its total R&D in 2006 declined to $710 million from $892 million in 2005, its R&D in its "Consumer Digital Imaging Group" declined to $171 million from $179 million in 2005.[324]

In 2006, Kodak's worldwide employment declined to 40,900[325] from 51,100 in 2005. In 2006 its US employment declined to 20,600[326] from 25,500 in 2005.

Kodak's efforts to monetize its patent portfolio of intellectual property started to pay benefits. On December 29, 2006 it settled its patent infringement litigation with Sony Corporation. No money was then paid in the settlement according to Kodak's 2006 Form 10-K. The parties also entered into a cross-licensing agreement.[327]

Corporate governance issues concerning possible excessive concentration of power in one executive were not addressed by Kodak. As the result of Patricia Russo's abrupt resignation in 2001, Daniel Carp was (1) chairman of the board, (2) chief executive officer, (3) president, and (4) chief operating officer.[328] He held all four positions until 2003, when Antonio Perez became (1) president

---

324 Ibid, 10.

325 Ibid, 11.

326 Ibid, 11.

327 Ibid, 111.

328 See footnote 196, supra.

and (2) chief operating officer.[329] This power-sharing arrangement between CEO Carp and COO Perez continued through 2004.[330] After Antonio Perez became chairman of the board and chief executive officer in 2005, Kodak no longer had either a president or a chief operating officer.[331] In 2006 Antonio Perez was still chairman of the board and CEO without a president or chief operating officer. [332] There was no president or chief operating officer to say, "Maybe you should not do that. Maybe you should not outsource production of digital cameras. Maybe you should not sell the Health Group. Maybe Kodak shouldn't take on so much debt. Is this something George Eastman would have done?"

Kodak's cash decreased by $196 million from $1,665 million at the end of 2005 to $1,469 million at the end of 2006.[333] Its 2006 Form 10-K indicated that its long-term debt declined to $2,714 million in 2006 from $2,764 million the year before.[334] Its 2006 Form 10-K indicated that

---

329 Eastman Kodak Company, Form 10-K annual report for the year ended Dec. 31, 2003, 16.

330 Eastman Kodak Company, Form 10-K annual report for the year ended Dec. 31, 2004, 13.

331 See "EXECUTIVE OFFICERS OF THE REGISTRANT," Eastman Kodak Company, Form 10-K annual report for the year ended Dec. 31, 2005, 21.

332 See "EXECUTIVE OFFICERS OF THE REGISTRANT," Eastman Kodak Company, Form 10-K annual report for the year ended Dec. 31, 2006, 20.

333 Eastman Kodak Company, Form 10-K annual report for the year ended Dec. 31, 2006, 59.

334 Ibid, 77.

its pension and other postretirement liabilities increased to $3,964 million in 2006 from $3,476 million the year before.[335]

More than halfway through Kodak's two-year transformation, it is fair to ask whether or not it was working. Its Consumer Digital Imaging Group sales declined 9 percent in 2006, and earned only $1 million that year.[336] The lack of profitability was a far cry from its 2006 target of $350–$450 million.[337] Kodak had a net loss of $601 million or -$2.09 per share in 2006.[338] Its balance sheet was weakened. Kodak faced the twin tactical problems of profitably growing its digital business and of repairing its balance sheet. A sale of the Health Group business might help achieve both objectives.

The Health Group was one of Kodak's five business segments in 2006. It made traditional film and digital radiology products. Its sales had remained steady at about $2.5 billion in the last three years. Its earnings had declined from $484 million in 2004, to $370 million in 2005, to $278 million in 2006.[339] On January 10, 2007, Kodak announced the sale of the Health Group to a Canadian company for $2.35 billion. Kodak said it would use $1.15

---

335 Ibid, 77.

336 Ibid, 33.

337 See footnote 319, above.

338 Eastman Kodak Company, Form 10-K annual report for the year ended Dec. 31, 2006.

339 Ibid, 33.

billion to pay off its secured debt and the balance of $1.2 billion for corporate purposes. Kodak would use its tax loss carry-forwards from the past several unprofitable quarters to offset that $1.2 billion. A portion of that would probably be used to fund Kodak's expected foray into the highly competitive market for inkjet printers.[340] Standard & Poor's was not impressed. They kept Kodak on credit watch with negative implications.[341]

As Kodak prepared for the introduction of its new inkjet printer, it continued to restructure. CEO Perez told analysts that it would increase its layoffs by 2,000 and that its three year restructuring would cost $3.6 billion to $3.8 billion, up from its previous estimate of $3.4 billion. He also said that Kodak's three-year restructuring would be completed as planned in 2007.[342] The local newspaper in Rochester reported that Kodak would eliminate 3,000 jobs worldwide and quoted the CEO as saying, "I want it to stop this year. It will stop this year."[343]

Amid the restructuring crisis, Kodak was beginning to see some light at the end of the proverbial tunnel. When it reported its earnings for the fourth quarter of 2006, it finally achieved a profit due to the recognition

---

340 See "Sale Positions Kodak for Printer Push," The Wall Street Journal, Jan. 11, 2007, A11.

341 Eastman Kodak Company, Form 10-K annual report for the year ended Dec. 31, 2006, 61.

342 See "Kodak Sees More Job Cuts, Higher Restructuring Costs," The Wall Street Journal, February 7, 2007.

343 Rochester Democrat and Chronicle, February 9, 2007, 1A and 4A.

of a nonrecurring licensing fee of $123 million paid by Sony in settlement of its patent litigation. However, the good news was mixed with the bad. Kodak's sales of digital cameras declined 25 percent in the fourth quarter of 2006 from 2005 as it withdrew from the low-priced market for digital cameras.[344]

Kodak's losses continued to narrow in the first quarter of 2007. It reported a loss of -$.53 versus a loss of -$1.04 in 2006. However, the good news was mixed with the bad. Kodak's consumer digital group had a 14 percent decline in sales and $114 million loss.[345]

The restructuring process involved downsizing of not only employees but also of real estate. Kodak had invested about $1 billion in China, including a giant plant in Xiamen to produce roll film.[346] On May 2, 2007, it announced that it would sell its 20 buildings there for $40 million, close its Chinese film-sensitizing operation, and record a charge of $220 million for the sale of those Chinese buildings.[347] Its Rochester real estate had a different fate. On June 25, 2007, it announced it would use explosives to level Building 9 and 23 in Kodak Park.[348] On

---

344 See "Kodak Takes Hit in Film and Digital," *The Wall Street Journal,* February 1, 2007, B3.

345 See "Kodak's Loss Narrows as Spending, Costs Drop," *The Wall Street Journal,* May 7, 2007.

346 See footnote 141, supra.

347 See "Kodak Will Sell Plant in China, Take Write-off," Rochester *Democrat and Chronicle,* May 3, 2007.

348 Rochester *Democrat and Chronicle,* June 26, 2007.

September 26, 2007, it announced it would sell[349] 330 more acres of Kodak Park, leaving approximately 100 buildings, down from 212 buildings in the 1990s. The systematic downsizing of Kodak's real estate was reminiscent of the scene from the motion picture *Around the World in 80 Days,* in which the steamboat was stripped of its wooden parts for engine fuel. What, if anything, would remain?

Kodak put its hopes for a comeback squarely on its new inkjet printers. They were a technological marvel. Anyone who has old color photographs knows how they fade over time. Kodak's inkjet printers provided genuinely archival prints that would not fade for one hundred years. The cost per print was less than one-half of rival printers built by Hewlett-Packard.[350] However, their rival spent almost $1 billion on printer R&D each year[351] and had a worldwide market share of 33 percent.[352] In this David vs. Goliath contest, little Kodak had spent a mere $248 million on its entire Consumer Digital Imaging Group in 2007.[353] Also, Kodak's photo editing software bundled with the machines was criticized as awkward.[354] Had Kodak waited too long to market its inkjet printer?

349 Rochester *Democrat and Chronicle*, Sept. 27, 2007.

350 See "Kodak's Moment of Truth," *Business Week*, February 19, 2007, 42.

351 Ibid, 44

352 Ibid, 49.

353 Eastman Kodak Company, Form 10-K annual report for the year ended Dec. 31, 2007, 8.

354 See "Kodak Moments for Less," *Business Week*, May 14, 2007, 24.

Its CEO believed that Kodak's inkjet printers would produce billions of dollars in sales.[355] The real issue was the amount of profits, if any, which the printer sales would produce. Some analysts worried that price discounts would impede profits.[356]

In September 2007, Kodak finally got its president and Chief Operating Officer, Philip J. Faraci. He was a twenty-two year veteran of Hewlett-Packard, where he had worked in its inkjet group.[357] Kodak had gone without a president or chief operating officer for almost two years and nine months. During that time Kodak had eliminated thousands of workers, written off its film manufacturing in China, accumulated debt, suffered credit downgrades, sold its Health Group, sold land in Kodak Park, and demolished buildings.

During this turmoil Kodak seemed about to repeat its past mistakes of abandoning entire markets to competitors. Decades earlier it had abandoned the 35mm camera market to the Japanese. In 2007, it withdrew from the low-priced digital camera market. It also did not participate in the exploding market for cameras in cell telephones. Multi-megapixel photo sensors were routinely incorporated into cell telephones. Where was Kodak? Where were Kodak cell telephones? Why weren't

---

355 See "Kodak's Moment of Truth," *Business Week*, February 19, 2007, 44.

356 *The Value Line Investment Survey*, Aug. 31, 2007, 130.

357 Eastman Kodak Company, Form 10-K annual report for the year ended Dec. 31, 2007, 14.

Kodak inkjet printers bundled with Kodak cell telephone cameras?

At the end of 2007 Kodak bragged about the end of its long restructurings. Its Form 10-K annual report stated: "This year Kodak substantially completed a four-year corporate restructuring and our 2007 results begin to reflect the benefits."[358]

Kodak's fourth quarter sales increased 3.7 percent, and its earnings from continuing operations rose to $92 million against a 2006 loss of $15 million. Sales at Kodak's consumer digital group rose 17 percent, and Kodak said it sold 520,000 inkjet printers in 2007. Without making a specific earnings forecast, the CEO told analysts that Kodak would profitably grow in the future.[359]

Kodak's finances improved in 2007. While Standard & Poor's maintained its negative outlook, it removed Kodak from credit watch. Moody's raised Kodak's outlook from negative to stable.[360] Kodak's long-term debt declined to $1,289 million from $2,714 million in 2006. Its pension and other postretirement liabilities declined to $3,444 million from $3,934 million in 2006.[361]

---

358 Eastman Kodak Company, Form 10-K annual report for the year ended Dec. 31, 2007, 4.

359 See "Kodak's Fourth-Quarter Profit Soared," *The Wall Street Journal*, Jan. 31, 2008.

360 Eastman Kodak Company, Form 10-K annual report for the year ended Dec. 31, 2007, 35.

361 Ibid, 43.

In 2007 Kodak's worldwide employment declined to 26,900 people[362] from 40,900 in 2006. In 2007 its US employment declined to 14,200[363] from 20,600 in 2006.

R&D expenditures continued downward. Total R&D declined to $535 million in 2007 from $578 million in 2006. R&D attributed specifically to the Consumer Digital Imaging Group declined to $248 million in 2007 from $281 million in 2006.

Analysis of its Consolidated Statement of Operations shows that Kodak really lost money in 2007. Its loss from continuing operations before income taxes was –$256 million. This large loss was masked by a $51 million benefit for income taxes, and a credit of $881 million for earnings from discontinued operations. With the tax credit and the earnings from discontinued operations, Kodak was able to show net earnings in 2007 of $676 million, although it lost –$256 million from its continuing operations.[364]

The total compensation for Kodak's CEO Perez increased to $9,278,434 in 2007 from $8,776,110 in 2006. The total compensation for President and COO

---

362 Ibid, 8.

363 Ibid, 8.

364 Ibid, 42.

Faraci increased to $2,852,325 in 2007 from $1,571,537 in 2006.[365]

Kodak's restructuring had been "substantially completed" just in time for the 2008–2009 worldwide financial crisis.

---

365 Notice of 2008 Annual Meeting and Proxy Statement dated April 3, 2008, "Compensation of Named Executive Officers," 51.

POINT II

AFTER THE FINANCIAL CRISIS

8 - WAS THE RESTRUCTURING WORTH IT?
(2008–2011)

On January 30, 2008, Kodak announced that its Rochester area employment declined to 9,200 workers from 12,500 in 2007. Kodak, which had long dominated the Rochester economy, slipped to third place behind the University of Rochester and Wegmans Food Markets. In 1982, Kodak had employed about 60,000 workers in Rochester.[366]

The human toll of wrecked careers was only part of the price paid by Rochester for Kodak's transformation. Kodak's manufacturing complex, euphemistically named Kodak Park, was a source of major environmental pollution and chemical contamination. In 2004, there were more than 45,000 miles of pipes in Kodak Park, and over 400 acres of groundwater was polluted.[367] In 2007, Kodak had $55 million in expenditures for pollution, waste treatment, and site remediation. Kodak estimated it would take 28 years to investigate, monitor, and remediate its manufacturing properties. It estimated the future

---

366 See "Kodak slips to third place," Rochester *Democrat and Chronicle*, Jan. 31, 2008, 1A.

367 See "Huge cleanup ahead," Rochester *Democrat and Chronicle*, Aug. 22, 2004, 1A.

expenses at $125 million, and reported them as other longterm liabilities on its balance sheet.[368]

Kodak's never-ending layoffs harmed the Rochester economy. Near the end of 2003 office vacancies rose to record levels in downtown Rochester.[369] On March 3, 2004, unemployment hit a twenty-year high.[370] The Brookings Institution reported that salaries for upstate professionals were less than the national average.[371] Area bankruptcy petitions increased 6.8 percent to 5,562 in 2004.[372] Business confidence in Rochester in 2005 was the lowest in all of New York State.[373] On July 1, 2005, it was reported that Monroe County had the largest decline in population in fifteen years.[374] By the end of 2005 Standard & Poor's gave Monroe County the lowest credit rating in the state, with a Negative outlook.[375] Row after row of stores were vacant or boarded up on Main Street. With the exception of a small movie theater that showed independent movies, all motion picture theaters had moved out of downtown. On October 29, 2007, there was a day-

---

368 Eastman Kodak Company, Form 10-K annual report for the year ended Dec. 31, 2007, "Note 11: Commitments and Contingencies – Environmental," 63.

369 Rochester *Democrat and Chronicle*, Sept. 19, 2003.

370 Rochester *Democrat and Chronicle*, Mar. 4, 2004.

371 See "Upstate Salaries Lagging," Rochester *Democrat and Chronicle*, Sept. 14, 2004, 8D.

372 Rochester *Democrat and Chronicle*, Jan. 6, 2005, 8D.

373 Rochester *Democrat and Chronicle*, Mar. 6, 2005.

374 Rochester *Democrat and Chronicle*, Mar. 16, 2006.

375 Rochester *Democrat and Chronicle*, Dec. 26, 2005.

time gunfight at the corner near St. Paul Street and East Main Street in which a teenager was wounded.[376] As a result of this publicity, many people became afraid to go downtown, especially after dark. In contrast to the suburbs, downtown parking was expensive and inconvenient. The central shopping area known as Midtown Plaza closed and was to be demolished. The water reservoir at Cobbs Hill was contaminated and a boil-water advisory was issued.[377] High-income taxes drove wealthy residents away. A former gubernatorial candidate changed his domicile to Florida to save $13,800 a day in income taxes.[378] Violence and lawlessness reached a crescendo in 2010 when more than twelve police were called to end a fight involving more than one hundred teenagers near the intersection of Main Street and South Avenue.[379] Crowds of noisy and violent teenagers congregated each day at the Liberty Pole just when business workers were leaving for home.[380] In years past, small business tried to attract people downtown with the slogan, "I'd rather be in Rochester."

How could Kodak attract talented professionals and managers, if its hometown became Upstate New York's

---

376 Rochester *Democrat and Chronicle*, Oct. 30, 2007, 3B.

377 Rochester *Democrat and Chronicle*, Sept. 18, 2006, 1B.

378 Rochester *Democrat and Chronicle*, May 15, 2009, 1A.

379 Rochester *Democrat and Chronicle*, Jan. 22, 2010, 2B.

380 See photographs and article in Rochester *Democrat and Chronicle*, May 23, 2010.

version of a violent and decrepit third world city of the 1970s?

As Rochester tried to muddle through, Kodak became more and more enthusiastic about its own future. Kodak predicted it would sell between 1 million and 1.5 million inkjet printers in 2008, and that the printers would break even by 2010. It also forecast annual revenue gains of 5 percent through 2011 and that operating earnings would then be $1 billion. It predicted total sales of digital products would increase 10 percent to 12 percent per year through 2011.[381] With the benefit of hindsight, these predictions were a bet that there would be no recession in 2008 and 2009.

On June 24, 2008, Kodak received an income tax refund of $581 million from its 1994 sale of Sterling Drug. It decided to use the proceeds to fund a $1 billion stock buyback. After the announcement, Kodak stock increased $1.69 on the NYSE to $14.03. In less than four years, its stock would trade for less than $1 per share.

Some Kodak executives must have known that the inkjet printers were not selling well by the beginning of August 2008. On the first day of that month, the company announced it would cut retiree health, dental, and

---

381 See "Kodak Forecasts Increase in Revenue, Pinning Optimism on Inkjet Printers," *The Wall Street Journal*, February 8, 2008.

life insurance. As usual, Kodak did this under the pretext of staying competitive.[382]

Kodak had a history of intentionally reducing employee health-care costs. As early as 1995, it had used its market power to negotiate lower premiums for its employees.[383] The next step was introduction of a self-insurance plan for some of its employees in 1997. On Sept 21, 2001, Kodak announced that in 2002 it would offer only self-insured health-care coverage to its Rochester workers.[384] The result was to remove almost 35,000 workers from the local Blue Cross and Preferred Care pool of workers, thereby increasing health-care premiums for non-Kodak Rochester workers.[385] This action was promptly copied by Kodak's crosstown rival, Xerox Corporation, which announced that in 2002 it would self-insure its 12,150 Monroe County employees.[386] This meant higher health-care costs for small businesses in the Rochester area.[387] Not to be outdone by Kodak and Xerox, the University of Rochester announced that beginning on July 1, 2002,

---

382 See "Kodak Cuts Retiree Benefits," Rochester *Democrat and Chronicle,* Aug. 1, 2008, 1A.

383 See footnote 63, supra.

384 See "Kodak Opts for Self-insurance," Rochester *Democrat and Chronicle,* Sept. 22, 2001, 12D.

385 Ibid.

386 Rochester *Democrat and Chronicle,* "Xerox Will Self-insure Health Plans in Monroe," Oct. 9, 2001.

387 See "Paying a Premium," Rochester *Democrat and Chronicle,* Oct. 14, 2001.

it would self-insure its 12,690 employees.[388] Thus, a total of 59,840 workers in the Rochester area would be self-insured by the middle of 2002. The result was massive increases in health-care premiums for members of Blue Cross and Preferred Care. For example, the premiums for Blue Cross increased 19 percent in 2001, 12.5 percent in 2002, 12.9 percent in 2003, 7.7 percent in 2004, and 14.5 percent in 2005.[389] While the process of increasing health-care premiums would probably have happened in the ordinary course of events, it was started and intensified by Kodak. But even self-insurance was not effective in controlling its health-care costs. Costs continued to increase until, in 2010, it was feared that some Kodak employees and retirees could suffer triple-digit percentage increases.[390] The ultimate solution to controlling health-care costs would be bankruptcy.

Kodak used its reduced retiree benefits to shield its earnings in the third quarter of 2008. While its net income tripled to $96 million from $37 million in 2007, its total sales fell 5 percent, and its digital operations had earnings of only $23 million on $820 million in sales. On the announcement, Kodak stock fell to $10.22

---

388 See "UR opts for self-insurance," Rochester *Democrat and Chronicle*, Mar. 26, 2002, 1A.

389 See "Health Insurance Hike Likely Here," Rochester *Democrat and Chronicle*, Sept. 24, 2005, 12D.

390 See "12,000 Kodak Employees and Thousands More Retirees Might Pay Much More for Health Care in 2010," Rochester *Democrat and Chronicle*, Oct. 30, 2009, 1A.

on the NYSE.[391] The announcement also hinted at new layoffs.[392]

On December 10, 2008, Kodak withdrew its full-year 2008 sales and profit forecast. Kodak stock declined to $6.59 on the NYSE.[393]

Analysts started to publicly question Kodak's accounting. Kodak's buyback was criticized for artificially lifting earnings per share by reducing the number of outstanding shares without changing operating earnings. [394] From June 24, 2008, through December 31, 2008, Kodak had spent $301 million to repurchase about 20 million shares at an average price of $15.01 per share.[395] The $301 million could have been better spent. In 2008, Kodak's stock repurchase had lost more than 50 percent of its $301 million investment.

At the end of 2008 Kodak no longer bragged about the end of its long restructurings. Its Form 10-K annual report stated,

As the company entered the second half of 2008, the global recession broadened dramatically and began to negatively impact all of its businesses. As a result, the

---

391 See "Kodak Sees Sales Falling; Plan New Round of Cuts," *The Wall Street Journal*, Oct. 31, 2008.

392 Ibid.

393 AP, "Eastman Kodak Withdraws Full-year 2008 Forecast," Wednesday, Dec. 10, 2008, 6:37 p.m. ET.

394 See "Quality Control," *Forbes*, Jan. 12, 2009, 49.

395 Eastman Kodak Company, Form 10-K annual report for the year ended Dec. 31, 2008, 21.

Company formulated the actions *necessary to align the business with the external realities.*[396] [emphasis added]

The company repeated a similar phrase as part of its "key priorities for 2009": "*Align the Company's cost structure with external economic realities.*"[397] [emphasis added]

The clear implication of "aligning with external realities" was that the prior restructurings had not gone far enough. Downsizing, layoffs, cost-cuttings, and benefit reductions would continue, if not intensify, in 2009.

Kodak's finances worsened in 2008. Standard & Poor's put Kodak back on its credit watch on November 3, 2008, and on December 3, 2008, lowered the ratings on Kodak's debt. Moody's put Kodak's ratings on review for a possible downgrade on December 12, 2008. The downgrade occurred on February 10, 2009.[398]

In the "Credit Quality" section of its annual report, Kodak warned,

Based on the Company's current financial forecasts, it is reasonably likely that the Company could breach its financial covenants in the first quarter of 2009 unless an appropriate amendment or waiver is obtained.[399]

---

396 Ibid, 4.
397 Ibid, 4.
398 Ibid, 44-45.
399 Ibid, 45.

In 2008, Kodak's worldwide employment declined to 24,400[400] from 26,900 in 2007. In 2008 its US employment declined to 12,800[401] from 14,200 in 2007.

In 2008 total R&D declined to $501 million from $549 million in 2007, according to its Form 10-K.[402] There was a discrepancy in total 2007 R&D between its 2008 10-K ($549 million)[403] and its 2007 10-K ($535 million).[404] What accounted for the $14 million difference?

In 2008, R&D attributed specifically to the Consumer Digital Imaging Group declined to $215 million from $250 million in 2007, according to its Form 10-K.[405] There was a discrepancy in CDIG 2007 R&D between its 2008 Form 10-K ($250 million)[406] and its 2007 Form 10-K ($248 million).[407] What accounted for the $2 million difference?

In 2008 its loss from continuing operations before income taxes increased to −$874 million from −$256 million in 2007.[408] This larger loss was masked by a $147 million benefit for income taxes and a credit of $285 million

---

400 Ibid, 9.

401 Ibid, 9.

402 Ibid, 8.

403 Ibid, 8.

404 Eastman Kodak Company, Form 10-K annual report for the year ended Dec. 31, 2007, 8.

405 Eastman Kodak Company, Form 10-K annual report for the year ended Dec. 31, 2008, 8.

406 Ibid, 8.

407 Eastman Kodak Company, Form 10-K annual report for the year ended Dec. 31, 2007, 8.

408 Eastman Kodak Company, Form 10-K annual report for the year ended Dec. 31, 2008, 28.

of earnings from discontinued operations, so that Kodak was able to show a net loss of –$442 million in 2008, even though its operations actually lost –$874 million.[409]

The total compensation for Kodak's CEO Perez decreased to $8,636,628 in 2008 from $9,278,434 in 2007. The total compensation for President and COO Faraci decreased to $1,797,501 in 2008 from $2,852,325 in 2007.[410]

There are discrepancies in the 2008 amounts of executive compensation in the 2009 and 2010 Proxies. For President and COO Faraci, the 2008 total compensation listed in the 2009 Proxy Statement was $1,797,501[411]; his 2008 total compensation listed in the 2010 Proxy Statement was $2,593,251.[412] For 2009 his compensation almost *doubled* to $4,599,518.[413] For CEO Perez, the 2008 total compensation listed in the 2009 Proxy Statement was $8,636,628[414]; his 2008 total compensation listed in the 2010 Proxy Statement was $7,825,088.[415] For 2009

---

409 Ibid, 29.

410 Notice of 2009 Annual Meeting and Proxy Statement dated April 2, 2009, "Compensation of Named Executive Officers," 49.

411 Ibid, 49.

412 Notice of 2010 Annual Meeting and Proxy Statement dated April 1, 2010, 61.

413 Ibid, 61.

414 Notice of 2009 Annual Meeting and Proxy Statement dated April 2, 2009, 49.

415 Notice of 2010 Annual Meeting and Proxy Statement dated April 1, 2010, 61.

the CEO's compensation *increased by about 60 percent* to $12,625,319.[416]

In summary, the 2010 Proxy Statement reported that the top two Kodak executives received substantial pay increases in 2009. For President Faraci, the increase was $2,007,267. For CEO Perez the increase was $4,800,231. The total increase in executive compensation in 2009 for Kodak's top two executives was $6,807,498.

While the top two executives were getting pay raises in 2009, Kodak suspended its dividend, stopped producing Kodachrome, and suffered debt downgrades. What happened to the George Fisher reforms that linked pay to performance? Is this something George Eastman would have done? Would George Eastman have taken a raise while Eastman Kodak Company was in financial trouble?

On February 4, 2009, Kodak said it anticipated a 2009 loss from continuing operations in the range of $400 million to $600 million and that 2009 sales would decline at least 12 percent. As analysts and investors worried about Kodak's cash position and debt, the value of its shares declined to $4.19 on the NYSE.[417]

On March 5, 2009, Standard & Poor's downgraded Kodak's debt to junk status on worries about its negative

---

416 Ibid, 61.

417 See "Kodak Fails to Calm Skeptical Investors," *The Wall Street Journal*, February 5, 2009.

cash flow. The value of its shares declined to $2.45 on the NYSE.[418]

On April 30, 2009, Kodak announced that its first quarter loss tripled to $353 million and that its sales declined 29 percent. It would save cash by laying off 3,500 to 4,500 employees in 2009. It also suspended its dividend.[419] The suspension of the dividend would save Kodak about $135 million per year.[420]

On June 22, 2009, Kodak announced it was discontinuing Kodachrome. Introduced in 1935, it was a color slide film, whose transparencies were either viewed on a flat light box, or projected onto silver-coated viewing screens. Its archival qualities—resistance to fading— made it the choice of many amateur and professional photographers.[421]

On July 7, 2009, CEO Perez predicted that growth would not return for about two more years.[422]

---

418 See "S&P Downgrades Eastman Kodak, Citing Cash Burn," AP, Friday, March 6, 2009, 7:18 a.m. ET.

419 See "Kodak Posts Wider 1Q Loss, Suspends Dividend," AP, Thursday, April 30, 2009, 8:56 a.m. EDT.

420 The Value Line Investment Survey, May 29, 2009, 123.

421 See "Kodak to Take Kodachrome Away," The Wall Street Journal, June 23, 2009.

422 See "Kodak CEO Bets Big on Printers," The Wall Street Journal, July 8, 2009, B6.

On July 30, 2009, Kodak reported second quarter results. It lost –$189 million during the second quarter, and its sales declined 29 percent.[423]

On October 29, 2009, Kodak reported third quarter results. It lost –$111 million during the third quarter, and its sales declined 26 percent.[424]

On September 16, 2009, Kodak resorted to nonbank financing to obtain about $700 million in new financing. First, it got a commitment from private equity firm KKR (Kohlberg Kravis Roberts & Co.) to purchase up to $400 million in new senior secured notes and warrants to buy up to 53 million shares. Second, it would offer $300 million in new senior convertible notes to institutional investors.[425]

Kodak hoped this financing would help it survive the 2009 losses until its business recovered. But would its business recover enough? How many quarters of growth would prove that its recovery was real? How long would its recovery last? Would a single decent quarter prove that most of Kodak's problems were solved? Was a single decent quarter the result of operations or of non-recurring patent lawsuits? Some investors forgot these

---

423 See "Eastman Kodak Posts 2Q Loss, Sales and Shares Drop," AP, July 30, 2009, 5:36 p.m. EDT.

424 See "Kodak Posts Fourth Straight Quarterly Loss," AP, 8:26 a.m. EDT, Thursday, Oct. 29, 2009.

425 See "Eastman Kodak in Deal with KKR to Raise Capital," AP, Wednesday, Sept. 18, 2009, 6:13 p.m. EDT.

questions, and were quick to forgive everything at any sign of a turnaround.

Kodak's 2009 fourth quarter earnings were announced on January 28, 2010. Kodak earned $443 million against a loss of −$918 million in 2008. Sales rose 6 percent, and digital sales rose 12 percent. Its stock rose to $5.92 on the NYSE. During a conference call CEO Perez stated, "Our strategy is working."[426]

Kodak's CEO Perez was quoted in the local newspaper saying, "We are starting 2010 with the best momentum possible—the best momentum I can remember with the company."[427]

On February 11, 2010, Standard & Poor's, while maintaining its ratings on Kodak's debt, raised its outlook from negative to stable.[428]

Kodak quickly raised the 2009 pay of its top two executives by $6,807,498.[429] It also restored the 3.5 percent wage bonus for its workers that it had cut in 2009.[430]

426 See "Kodak Posts 1st Quarterly Profit in More Than Year," AP, Thursday, Jan. 28, 2010, 4:40 p.m. EST.

427 Rochester Democrat and Chronicle, February 5, 2010, "Kodak Sets Sights on Digital Expansion," 1A.

428 See "S & P Lifts Outlook on Eastman Kodak to 'Stable'," AP, Thursday, February 11, 2010, 5:03 p.m. EST.

429 See footnotes 411–416, supra.

430 See "Kodak Bonuses Restored," Rochester Democrat and Chronicle, February 6, 2010, 1A.

Lost in this euphoria were two important facts. First, despite the alleged progress in 2009's fourth quarter, Kodak lost money for the year. Second, the fourth quarter was helped by a $414 million licensing payment from Korean company LG. Kodak expected to receive a $550 million payment from Korean company Samsung in 2010. Some analysts were skeptical that Kodak's turnaround would last.[431]

The 2009 compensation of Kodak's CEO was criticized as excessive and not linked to his company's performance. According to pay expert Graef Crystal, Kodak's CEO Perez was overpaid by $9.29 million. Kodak had amended the CEO's employment contract to accelerate a $6.18 million stock award that had been scheduled for 2009. As Kodak lost $210 million in 2009, and as its stock lost one-third of its value, its CEO's compensation had increased 61 percent.[432] Is this something George Eastman would have done?

Analysis of Kodak's 2009 Form 10-K indicates the real importance of the $414 million LG settlement. Under "DETAILED RESULTS OF OPERATIONS," Kodak listed Consumer Digital Imaging Group 2009 sales of $2,619 million, a decline of 15 percent from 2008.[433] Are law-

---

431 *Barron's, February 8, 2010, M5.*

432 *Bloomberg.com,* "CBS Overpaid Moonves $28 Million in Study of Chief Executives," May 6, 2010.

433 Eastman Kodak Company, Form 10-K annual report for the year ended Dec. 31, 2009, 29.

suit settlements sales? Under the heading of "Other Operating (Income) Expenses, Net" Kodak gave details of the LG settlement. As part of the settlement, Kodak sold its organic light emitting diodes (OLED) group to LG for $100 million, which was allocated to the asset sale:

> The remaining gross proceeds of $414 million were allocated to the licensing transaction and *reported in net sales of the CDG segment.*"[434] [emphasis added]

Thus, the reported sales of the CDG group included $414 million of settlement money. Had this money been subtracted from the CDG 2009 sales, the real sales would have been as follows:

$2,619 million

– $414 million

$2,205 million

In 2009 Kodak's worldwide employment declined to 20,250 people[435]from 24,400 in 2008. Its US employment declined to 10,630 people[436] from 12,800 in 2008.

In 2009 its total R&D declined to $356 million from $478 million in 2008, and its CDIG R&D declined to $146 million from $205 million in 2008.[437]

---

434 Ibid, 32.

435 Ibid, 8.

436 Ibid, 8.

437 Ibid, 8.

In 2009 Kodak's net sales declined 19 percent to $7,606 million from $9,416 million in 2008.[438] In 2009 Kodak had a net loss from continuing operations, before income taxes, of −$117 million as opposed to −$874 million in 2008.[439]

According to the ratings companies, Kodak's financial position improved in 2009. On February 11, 2010, Standard & Poor's raised Kodak's outlook from negative to stable. On February 19, 2010 Moody's raised Kodak's outlook from negative to stable.[440] Nevertheless, Kodak's financial dealings in 2009 had exposed its common stock shareholders to potential dilution of their interest. The $400 million of 7 percent convertible notes, which it issued on September 23, 2009, were convertible at an initial rate of 134.9528 shares per $1,000 principal of notes.[441] Hence, potentially the notes could be converted into 400,000 additional shares. As part of its sale of senior secured notes sold to KKR, Kodak had issued Warrants to purchase 40 million shares at $5.50 per share.[442] Thus, the total potential dilution to common shareholders was 40,400,000 shares. As of December 31, 2009, Kodak had

---

438 Ibid, 29.
439 Ibid, 30.
440 Ibid, 49.
441 Ibid, 48.
442 Ibid, 47.

268,630,514 shares outstanding.[443] The potential dilution was 15 percent.

Kodak reported its second consecutive quarterly profit on April 29, 2010. It earned $119 million (or $.40 per share) against a year earlier loss of -$360 million (-$1.34 per share). Its shares declined $1.15 on the NYSE to $7.20 because it gave guidance of a full-year 2010 loss of -$50 million to -$150 million.[444]

The losses resumed in the next quarter. Although its revenue from its inkjet printers increased by 50 percent, it lost -$.63 per share in 2010's second quarter.[445] Demand for motion picture film was reduced by the digitalization of motion picture studios. Sales of Kodak's digital cameras also declined. During the earnings conference call, the CEO acknowledged competition from smart phone cameras, but added, "There's room for both."[446]

With no Kodak cell phone camera of its own, its corporate response to competition from phone cameras was basically limited to intellectual property lawsuits. In 2008 Kodak had set a goal of receiving $250 million to $350 million per year through 2011 from its intellectual

---

443 Ibid, 56- See "Consolidated Statement of Financial Position."

444 *MarketWatch*, April 29, 2010, 11:54 a.m., EDT.

445 AP, Wednesday, July 28, 2010, 8:15 a.m.

446 See *The Wall Street Journal*, "Fresh Kodak Concerns Surface," July 29, 2010, B5.

property. In 2010, the goal was extended one year to 2012.[447] Is this something George Eastman would have done? Would George Eastman have manufactured Kodak cell phone cameras, or would he have sued other companies for allegedly stealing Kodak's ideas?

Kodak continued to rely heavily on its intellectual property in its third quarter of 2010. It added about $210 million in gross quarterly profit from a licensing deal with an undisclosed rival. Nevertheless, it still lost −$43 million or −$.16 per share.[448] While Kodak's press release put a positive spin on the results,[449] others still had doubts. As Kodak's Chief Financial Officer announced his plans to move to Tyco International on December 1, 2010, Fitch Ratings lowered Kodak's outlook from stable to negative. In particular, a Fitch director stated, "When you back out IP revenue, the remaining businesses are marginally profitable, if at all."[450]

Other analysts thought Kodak would continue to lose money.[451]Kodak shares had fallen almost 80 percent in

---

447 See *The Wall Street Journal*, "At Kodak, Patents Hold the Key to the Future," April 20, 2010, and *The Wall Street Journal*, "Kodak Chief Perez Plans to Curtail Patent Lawsuits," June 25, 2010.

448 AP, "Kodak Posts Narrower 3Q Loss of $43," Thursday, Oct. 28, 2010, 2:32 p.m.

449 "Kodak Reports Improved Profits and Cash Flow in Third Quarter 2010," Thursday, Oct. 28, 2010, 6:52 a.m. EDT.

450 See "Fitch Cuts Kodak Outlook," *The Wall Street Journal*, Oct. 13, 2010.

451 *The Value Line Investment Survey*, Nov. 26, 2010, 118.

market value since Perez became CEO.[452] Would Kodak recover its profitability in the fourth quarter of 2010? How would it perform during the holiday season?

On January 26, 2011, Kodak reported earnings fell 95 percent from $443 million or $1.40 per share in the fourth quarter of 2009 to $22 million or $.08 per share in 2010. Its digital sales fell 25 percent.[453] Kodak tried to put a positive spin on these disappointing results. The headline on its Press Release stated, "Kodak Reports Full-Year Revenue of $7.187 Billion, Full-Year 2010 Gross Profit *Improves*," [emphasis added].

In an interview on February 3, 2011, CEO Perez, when questioned about a bankruptcy filing or buyout, stated,

Absolutely not...I understand that some people say that. Why they say it, I don't want to make a judgment. There is no reason in the world to believe that we will be in that (position) in any scenario that we can imagine.[454]

Twenty-two days later, Kodak admitted that its 2010 loss was bigger than it previously reported. Kodak had previously reported a 2010 loss of −$70 million or −$.26

---

452 See "Some CEOs Face Big Repair Jobs in 2011," *The Wall Street Journal*, Jan. 4, 2011, B6.

453 AP, "Kodak 4Q Profit Drops 95pct, Misses Expectations," Wednesday, Jan. 26, 2011, 8:31 a.m.

454 AP, "CEO Antonio Perez Says Kodak's Turning Point Is 2012," Published Thursday, February 03, 2011, 9:20 a.m., Updated Thursday, February 03, 2011, 9:38 a.m.

per share. Due to a charge of $626 million, it now said it lost –$687 million or –$2.56 per share in 2010.[455]

As its operating results deteriorated, Kodak faced setbacks on the patent litigation front. The International Trade Commission ruled against Kodak in its patent infringement complaint against Apple and Research In Motion.[456] Some analysts began to publicly question the options for a Kodak bankruptcy or buyout.[457]

In 2010, Kodak's reliance on intellectual property settlements more than doubled. The 2009 Form 10-K had applied $414 million of intellectual property settlement monies toward CDG sales.[458] In 2010, Kodak applied non-recurring intellectual property licensing agreements of $838 million toward CDG revenues.[459] Total revenues of the Consumer Digital Imaging Group in 2010 were $2,739 million.[460] Since $838 million of that amount was licensing money, about 31 percent of 2010 digital revenues were not real sales of products, but were intellectual property licenses. Should all or even part of that

---

455 AP, "Big Charge Boosts Size of Eastman Kodak 2010 Loss," Friday, February 25, 2011, 1:06 p.m. EST.

456 See "ITC Rules for Apple, RIM against Kodak," *The Wall Street Journal,* Jan. 25, 2011.

457 See "Analysis: Investors Tired of Waiting for Kodak to Develop," Reuters, February 16, 2011.

458 See footnote 434, supra.

459 Eastman Kodak Company, Form 10-K annual report for the year ended Dec. 31, 2010, 31.

460 Ibid, 31.

$838 million, which was essentially nonrecurring, been recognized as revenues?

According to Kodak's 2010 Form 10-K, its net loss increased from –$210 million or –$.78 per share in 2009 to –$687 million or –$2.56 per share in 2010.[461] Kodak's loss from continuing operations (before income taxes) increased to –$561 million from –$117 million in 2009.[462]

In 2010, Kodak's R&D declined from $356 million in 2009 to $321 million. However, its Consumer Digital Imaging Group R&D actually increased R&D spending to $148 million from $146 million in 2009.[463]

In 2010, Kodak's worldwide employment declined to 18,800[464] from 20,250 in 2009. Its US employment declined to 9,600[465] from 10,630 people in 2009.

One hundred dollars invested in Kodak stock on December 31, 2005, would have declined in price to $24.81 on December 31, 2010, while the S&P 500 index would have increased to $111.99.[466] Kodak stock declined in price by –75.19 percent over that five-year period. This

---

461 Ibid, 35.
462 Ibid, 95.
463 Ibid, 7.
464 Ibid, 8.
465 Ibid, 8.
466 Ibid, 19.

is an average yearly stock price decline of about −15 percent per year.

On January 26, 2011, S&P put Kodak on Credit Watch with a Negative Outlook and a B− rating.[467] On February 28, 2011, S&P cut Kodak's credit rating to CCC, due to worries about its leverage and cash flow.[468] On March 3, 2011, Moody's cut Kodak's long-term debt rating to Caa1, with a negative outlook, due to worries about its cash burn rate.[469]

Kodak's Notice of 2011 Annual Meeting and Proxy Statement was dated March 31, 2011. The largest shareholder was Legg Mason with 51,920,124 shares. The second largest shareholder was KKR Fund Holdings L.P., with 40,000,000 shares.[470] According to the "Summary Compensation Table," CEO Perez's compensation declined from $12,625,319 in 2009 to $5,718,190 in 2010, and President Faraci's compensation declined from $4,599,518 in 2009 to $1,416,510 in 2010.[471]

In first quarter of 2011, Kodak's results continued their downward spiral. Sales declined 31 percent, it had

---

467 Ibid, 38.

468 *Reuters*, New York, February 28, 2011.

469 AP, March 3, 2011, 3:52 p.m. EST.

470 Notice of 2011 Annual Meeting and Proxy Statement, Mar. 31, 2011, 30.

471 Ibid, 49.

an operating loss of –$1.13 per share from continuing operations, and its stock fell to $2.89 on the NYSE.[472]

Kodak used a three-pronged strategy to deal with the crisis. First, it continued to sell off parts of the company in order to raise cash. On April 5, 2011, it sold parts of its microfilm business to Eastman Park Micrographics, Inc. for an undisclosed price.[473] Second, it sought to enhance its access to cash. On March 9, 2011, it announced a $200 million private placement of senior secured notes.[474] It also closed on a five-year credit agreement, giving it access to a maximum of $400 million.[475] Third, it modified its intellectual property strategy from litigation-only to sale of part or all of the patents.

On March 25, 2011, the US International Trade Commission announced it would review a judge's findings that cell phones from Apple and RIM did not violate an image-preview patent held by Kodak.[476] CEO Perez alleged that a Kodak victory could be worth more than

---

472 *Reuters*, April 28, 2011, 8:57 a.m. EDT.

473 See Press Release, "Kodak Sells Microfilm Unit to Eastman Park Micrographics," Tuesday, April 5, 2011, 4:01 p.m. EDT.

474 See Press Release, "Kodak Launches Private Placement of $200 Million Senior Secured Notes," Wednesday, March 9, 2011, 7:14 a.m. EST.

475 See Press Release, "Kodak Closes on Amended and Restated Credit Agreement, Enhances Financial Flexibility," Tuesday, April 26, 2011, 4:05 p.m.

476 *AP*, March 25, 2011, 8:10 p.m. EDT.

$1 billion.[477] On May 18, 2011, third party investigators at the ITC found that Apple and RIM infringed on Kodak's image preview patent and recommended barring imports of their cell phones.[478] However, the ITC partially ruled against Kodak on July 1, 2011, and sent the case back to the judge.[479]

While the Apple and RIM litigation was moving in an inconclusive direction, Kodak sold 850 image sensor patents and patent applications to OmniVision, a maker of image sensors for cell phones. The price was $65 million.[480] This was the first time in memory that Kodak had sought to profit from its intellectual property portfolio from an outright sale as opposed to lawsuit verdicts and settlements. It was the beginning of Kodak's efforts to sell its patent portfolio.

Some investors decided not to wait for any further patent sales. Legg Mason sold 18.2 million Kodak shares

---

477 *Bloomberg.com,* "Kodak Says $1 Billion at Stake in Apple, RIM Patent Dispute," Mar. 25, 2011, also see *AP,* "Kodak Up after Recommendation in Patent Battle," Wednesday, May 18, 2011, 6:13 p.m. EDT.

478 *AP,* May 18, 2011, 6:13 p.m. EDT.

479 *Bloomberg.com,* "Kodak's Patent Case against Apple, RIM Left Unresolved by ITC," July 1, 2011.

480 *AP,* "OmniVision Buys Eastman Kodak Patents for $65 Million," April 1, 2011 5:44 p.m. EDT.

at a $551 million loss.[481] By November, 2011 Legg Mason had sold the rest of its stock.[482]

As financial analysts questioned whether or not Kodak's pension obligations were underfunded,[483] Kodak's bonds also went in a southerly direction. By July 18, 2011, its 2013 bonds yielded more than 16 percent.[484]

On July 26, 2011, Kodak announced its second quarter results. It reported a loss of –$179 million or –$.67 per share as opposed to a loss of –$167 million or –$.62 the year earlier.[485]

The title of Chapter 8 of this book posed a question: Was the Restructuring Worth It? In view of the evidence provided, the answer should be self-evident. Nothing was done that prevented Kodak's descent into bankruptcy.

---

481 *Bloomberg.com*, "Legg Mason's Miller Sells Kodak Stake," June 28, 2011.

482 *The Wall Street Journal, WSJ.com*, "Bill Miller Is Done Losing Money on Kodak," Nov. 10, 2011, 6:33 p.m. ET.

483 *Forbes.com*, " *Great Speculations—Eastman Kodak Looking Like A Zombie Stock*," Mar. 22, 2011, 1:15 p.m.

484 *The Wall Street Journal*, "Kodak's Bonds Fading Fast," July 19, 2011.

485 Press Release, "Kodak Reports 2nd Quarter Results; Key Growth Businesses Continue to Gain Momentum," July 26, 2011, 7:02 a.m. EDT.

9 - To Bankruptcy Court
(2011–2012)

By the summer of 2011, Kodak faced the unpleasant choice of either selling the company itself or selling its patents. Kodak adopted a poison-pill plan to make a company sale unlikely. If a new investor acquired at least 4.9 percent of Kodak's stock, the company would issue current investors one "preferred share right" for each share of common stock then owned. Hence, new investors would be subject to significant dilution of their ownership interest.[486] After the announcement, Kodak shares declined to $2.37 on the NYSE.[487]

While Kodak explored the sale of part of its patent portfolio, its cash burn problems intensified. By March 31, 2011, Kodak's cash had declined by $300 million to $1.3 billion. $50 million of debt was due in 2011, $50 million of debt was due in 2012, and $300 million of debt

---

486 -See Press Release, "Kodak Adopts Plan to Preserve Valuable Net Operating Losses," Aug. 1, 2011, 8:00 a.m. EDT.

487 See *Bloomberg.com*, "Kodak Board Adopts Plan to Block Takeovers," Aug. 1, 2011.

was due in 2013.[488] In its press release announcing that Kodak had retained Lazard, LLC as its advisor to assist in the sale of about 10 percent of its patent portfolio, Kodak stated,

> Kodak *invented the digital camera* and since then has pioneered many of the major advances in digital imaging devices, systems and services.[489] [emphasis added]

Kodak's plan to sell part of its patents backfired. It made the company look more valuable dead than alive. According to an analysis by Bloomberg, Kodak's pension plans were underfunded at the end of 2010 by $1.21 billion, and the company itself had equity value of only $600 million. In contrast, its patent portfolio might be worth as much as $3 billion.[490] This made Kodak look attractive as a merger candidate. A large shareholder publicly urged Kodak to sell itself.[491]

According to Kodak's CEO, numerous potential buyers contacted the company about buying its patents.[492] Some experts questioned the value of the patents,

---

488 See *The Wall Street Journal*, "Kodak Considers Sale of Digital-Photo Patents," July 21, 2011.

489 See Press Release, "Kodak Exploring Strategic Alternatives for Fundamental Digital Imaging Patent Portfolios," July 20, 2011, 8:07 a.m.

490 See *Bloomberg.com*, "Kodak Worth Five Times More in Breakup With $3 Billion Patents: Real M&A," Aug. 16, 2011.

491 See *Reuters.com*, "Investor Urges Kodak to Sell Itself," Sept. 29, 2011.

492 See *Bloomberg.com*, "Kodak Says Many Buyers Evaluating Patents," Aug. 30, 2011.

because many patents had already been licensed.[493] Other experts questioned their value because of carelessness in filing.[494]

The straw that broke the camel's back was Kodak's decision to draw $160 million from its $400 million bank credit line.[495] Moody's downgraded Kodak's debt,[496] and Fitch downgraded Kodak's debt to reflect probable default.[497]

Three unnamed people supposedly familiar with the marketing of the patents leaked a report to the financial press that Kodak was considering a bankruptcy filing. A Kodak spokesman stated:

> As we sit here today, the company has no intention of filing, and there is no change in our strategy to monetize our intellectual property.[498] [emphasis added]

This statement left open the intention of filing for bankruptcy at a later time. Some of the potential buyers

---

493 *The Wall Street Journal*, "Kodak Patent Sale Fuels Hopes That May Be Too High," Sept. 7, 2011.

494 See *Financial Times*, "Cash Call Sends Kodak Shares Down 25%," Sept. 26, 2011, 8:49 p.m.

495 See footnote 475, supra; and *Bloomberg.com*, "Kodak Draws $160M from Revolving Credit Line," Sept. 23, 2011.

496 *AP*, "Moody's Cuts Debt Ratings on Eastman Kodak," Sept. 27, 2011, 10:59 p.m. EDT.

497 *AP*, "Fitch Downgrades Debt Ratings on Kodak," September 28, 2011, 4:15 p.m. EDT.

498 *Businessweek.com*, "Kodak Said to Weigh Bankruptcy Filing to Spur Patent Sale," Sept. 30, 2011, 3:14 p.m. EDT.

feared that the patent sale could legally be a "fraudulent transfer" if Kodak were to subsequently file for bankruptcy.[499] Thus, the patent sale, which had been intended to provide Kodak with operating funds to avoid bankruptcy, ironically became the impetus for a bankruptcy filing. It also caused investors to focus on Kodak's cash flow problems. A delay in obtaining cash from the patent sale might cause liquidity problems. In order to protect themselves, a group of bondholders organized an informal committee and hired a law firm to protect their interest.[500] They then sent a letter to Kodak's board threatening to sue if the patents were sold for less than their fair market value.[501]

Kodak announced its third quarter results on November 3, 2011. It lost almost five times as much money in the third quarter of 2011 compared to the year before. The loss was −$222 million or −$.83 per share compared to −$43 million or −$.16 the year before. Revenues declined 17 percent, and its cash balance declined to $862 million.[502] In a filing with the Securities and Exchange Commission, Kodak warned it might have trouble staying

499 See *Bloomberg.com*, "Kodak Debt Swaps Soar as Camera Maker Said to Weigh Bankruptcy," Sept. 30, 2011.

500 *The Wall Street Journal*, "Kodak Tensions Rise," Oct. 24, 2011.

501 See *Bloomberg.com*, "Kodak Lenders Send Board Letter on Fiduciary Duty in Asset Sale," Oct. 27, 2011.

502 Press Release, "Kodak Reports 3rd Quarter 2011 Results, Steady Progress in Transformation," Nov. 3, 2011, 6:55 a.m. EDT.

in business. As a result, its 2017 bond traded at $.37 on the dollar, and its stock price fell to $1.12 on the NYSE.[503]

Unable to quickly sell its patents, Kodak tried to raise cash by selling other parts of the company. On November 7, 2011, it announced sale of its image sensor business for an undisclosed amount.[504] It put its Internet Kodak Gallery up for sale.[505] Just before Christmas, it announced sale of its gelatin business for an undisclosed amount.[506]

As a bankruptcy filing became more and more likely, several directors resigned from Kodak's board. On December 27, 2011, two directors who represented KKR resigned.[507] A third director resigned shortly thereafter.[508]

Although Kodak did not publicly admit that it was preparing to file a bankruptcy petition, a bankruptcy offered the company the opportunity to sharply reduce its legacy health-care costs.[509] Previously, Kodak had sought to reduce health-care costs by negotiating lower premiums for its employees, by self-insuring, and by increasing

---

503 *The Wall Street Journal*, "Squeeze Tightens on Kodak," Nov. 4, 2011, B2.

504 *Reuters*, "Kodak Sells Image Sensor Business to Platinum Equity," Nov. 7, 2011, 7:41 p.m. EST.

505 *The Wall Street Journal*, "Kodak's Online Gallery up for Sale," Nov. 18, 2011, B1.

506 *The Wall Street Journal*, "Kodak Reshuffles Decks," Dec. 23, 2011, B1.

507 *Reuters*, "Two Resign from Kodak Board; Represented KKR," Dec. 27, 2011.

508 *The Wall Street Journal*, "Kodak Loses a Third Director," Dec. 31, 2011.

509 *The Wall Street Journal*, "Kodak Shuffles Advisers as It Fights to Avoid Bankruptcy," Dec. 6, 2011.

premiums for employees and retirees.[510] Now, by the means of bankruptcy, it might be possible to legally abrogate its contractual obligations to provide health benefits for its retirees and employees.

On January 3, 2012, Kodak announced that it received a warning that its shares could be delisted from the NYSE.[511] In response to a report of an imminent bankruptcy filing, a company spokesman said that Kodak "does not comment on market rumor or speculation."[512]

On January 5, 2012, Moody's cut ratings on Kodak's debt due to "heightened probability of a bankruptcy."[513] Its stock declined to $.48 on the NYSE.[514]

Kodak did not file its bankruptcy petition in Rochester. Instead, it filed in the United States Bankruptcy Court, Southern District of New York—in New York City. In a press release, it announced that it and its domestic subsidiaries filed voluntary petitions for Chapter 11 Reorganization on January 19, 2012. Its press release also announced that it obtained an eighteen-month $950 million loan from Citigroup to enable it to continue to operate during Chapter 11.[515]

---

510 See footnotes 383–390, supra.

511 See Kodak Press Release, Jan. 3, 2012.

512 *The Wall Street Journal*, Jan. 4, 2012, 3:12 p.m. ET.

513 *Bloomberg*, "Kodak Holds Bankruptcy Talks with Citigroup," Jan. 13, 2012.

514 *Bloomberg*, "US Stock-Index Futures Decline on JP Morgan," Jan. 13, 2012.

515 See Press Release, "Eastman Kodak Company and its U.S. Subsidiaries Commence Voluntary Chapter 11 Business Reorganization," Jan. 19, 2012.

Its notice concerning its fifty largest unsecured creditors was filed January 22, 2012. The first creditor was "Kodak Pension Plan of the United Kingdom." Thedollar amount of the claim was "Undetermined." The filing appeared to indicate that Kodak sought to use American bankruptcy law to terminate the pensions of its retirees in the UK.[516] It also listed "Preferred Care, Inc." for "Employee Benefits" in the sum of $4,350,643.[517] Among listed retailers were the following:

1.	Walmart	$11,421,973.
2.	Target	$ 9,009,509.
3.	Best Buy	$ 8,397,115.
4.	Office Max	$ 4, 658,704.
5.	Staples	$ 3,182,484.
6.	CVS	$ 3,168,410.
7.	Amazon.com	$ 3,027,401.
8.	Office Depot	$ 2,899,193.
9.	Sam's Wholesale Club	$ 2,709,212. [518]

Kodak continued to terminate workers in Rochester. As of December 31, 2011, Kodak employed 5,100 workers in the Rochester area. As of May 3, 2012, it announced about 480 new layoffs. [519] It announced an additional 79 layoffs by mid-August. [520]

---

516 See Doc 80, Case 12-10202 alg.

517 Ibid

518 Ibid

519 democratandchronicle.com 10:28 a.m., May 3, 2012.

520 Innovationtrail.org, "79 More Layoffs at Kodak's Eastman Business Park," June 8, 2012.

Kodak's compensation of its two highest executive officers increased in 2011. CEO Perez's compensation increased from $5,718,190 in 2010 to $6,980,114 in 2011. President Faraci's compensation increased from $1,416,510 in 2010 to $2,742,522 in 2011. [521]

During 2009, CEO Perez was granted $218,396 for personal aircraft usage as part of his "All Other Compensation." [522] On January 1, 2011, this perquisite was restricted to a maximum of $100,000 annually for personal use. As of Kodak's bankruptcy filing, no more personal use of aircraft was permitted because Kodak terminated its aircraft leases as part of its filing.[523]

Kodak's sales declined 16 percent from $7,167 million in 2010 to $6,022 million in 2011.[524] Kodak's net loss increased from −$687 million in 2010 to −$764 million in 2011.[525] Revenues at its Consumer Digital Imaging Group (CDG) declined 36 percent from $2,731 million in 2010 to $1,739 million in 2011.[526] The CDG segment, which had shown a profit of $278 million in 2010, reported a loss of −$349 million in 2011. [527]

---

521 Eastman Kodak Company Form 10-K/A for the year ended Dec. 31, 2011, 33.

522 Notice of 2010 Annual Meeting and Proxy Statement dated April 1, 2010, 63.

523 Eastman Kodak Company Form 10-K/A for the year ended Dec. 31, 2011,31.

524 Eastman Kodak Company, Form 10-K annual report for the year ended Dec. 31, 2011, 32.

525 Ibid, 33.

526 Ibid, 38.

527 Ibid, 38.

Thus, as the compensation of Kodak's top two executives increased in 2011, Kodak's operational losses also increased. How much had really changed since Sept. 10, 1989 when the then top two executives had pay increases, while the Company's profitability declined?[528] Is this something George Eastman would have done?

In the five-year period from December 31, 2006, to December 31, 2011, Kodak's stock price declined −97.33 percent.[529] This is an average loss of −19.47 percent per year.

Kodak's R&D declined to $274 million in 2011 from $318 million in 2010. Its CDG R&D declined to $134 million in 2011 from $176 million in 2010.[530]

In 2011 Kodak's worldwide employment declined to 17,100 workers from 18,800 in 2010[531]. Its US employment declined to 8,350 workers from 9,600 in 2010.[532]

In order to reduce losses, Kodak did what was once unthinkable: it stopped making cameras. Is this something George Eastman would have done? Kodak had been in the camera business since 1888. Kodak's easy-to-use cameras had popularized photography. It had made

---

528 See Chapter 2, supra.

529 Eastman Kodak Company, Form 10-K Annual Report for the year ended Dec. 31, 2011, 25.

530 Ibid, 9.

531 Ibid, 9.

532 Ibid, 9.

box cameras, folding cameras, miniature cameras, 35mm cameras, instant cameras, and digital cameras. This all ended in February, 2012. While Kodak had invented the first digital camera in 1975,[533] it had profited from the invention primarily from licensing intellectual property. It was never able to continually dominate the digital camera business.[534]

Kodak also sought to reduce its losses by trying to lower its property tax assessments by 26 percent[535] and by trying to cut its health-care benefits for retirees. On February 27, 2012, Kodak's lawyers filed a motion to reduce or terminate post-1991 retiree health-care benefits. In part the motion stated,

> The Debtors estimate that their consolidated balance sheet liability for Retiree Medical and Survivor Benefits is approximately $1.223 billion. Without the modifications requested herein, the Debtors' aggregate annual cash cost to provide Retiree Medical and Survivor Benefits is estimated to be approximately $118 million. If the relief sought herein is granted, it would reduce the Debtors' consolidated balance sheet liability for Retiree Medical and Survivor Benefits by

---

533 See *AP*, "Kodak to Stop Making Cameras, Digital Frames," Feb. 10, 2012; and *The Wall Street Journal*, "Kodak Shutters Camera Business," Feb. 10, 2012.

534 For photographs and descriptions of Kodak cameras, see *McKeown's Price Guide to Antique & Classic Cameras, 12th edition, 2005-2006, 472-536.*

535 See "Kodak Wants Property Assessments Lowered,"www.13wham.com/news/local/ story/Kodak-Wants-City-Property-Assessments-Lowered, June 4, 2012, 1:32 p.m.

approximately $223 million, resulting in annual cash savings of approximately $13.7 million for fiscal 2012, and approximately $20.5 million for each fiscal year thereafter.[536]

After objections from the retirees,[537] Kodak withdrew its motion,[538] and a retiree committee was formed to represent Kodak's 56,000 retirees.[539]

While Kodak was trying to cut its property taxes and trying to cut its retirees' health-care benefits, it asked the bankruptcy court to authorize bonuses for its executives. It asked the court for permission to pay up to $8.82 million in executive bonuses as incentive to successfully restructure the company.[540]

The motion for bonuses in part stated,

Moreover, Kodak *has demonstrated its commitment to a pay-only-for-performance philosophy.* In light of performance results, *no cash bonuses were paid to senior management for the 2011 performance year,* and *no cash payments were made under the company's long-term incentive programs...*[541] [emphasis added].

536 12-10202-alg, Document 432, 2, at paragraph 1.

537 See Document 570.

538 See Document 872.

539 See "Kodak Retirees Fight Proposal to End Health Benefits," *Bloomberg.com*, *"Lehman, Dynegy, Kodak, Ocala Funding, Cocopah: Bankruptcy, July 11, 2012.*

540 See *The Wall Street Journal*, "Bonuses Sought for Kodak Brass," July 12, 2012.

541 12-10202-alg, Document 1625, paragraph 5.

While no cash bonuses were paid in 2011, the executive compensation increased for Kodak's two top executives $2,587,936 as Kodak's net loss increased. [542] For what performance, if any, was the compensation increased in 2011?

The 2011 results of Fujifilm Holdings indicated a profit of $.75 per share in 2011, a dividend of $.43 per share in 2011, and a long-term debt of only 6 percent of capital as of April 27, 2012. [543] While it also laid off thousands of employees, it was able to transition to a post-film world by using its expertise to enter related non-film markets. [544]

Kodak's emergence from bankruptcy would materially depend on its ability to sell successfully its patent portfolio. Kodak claimed the patents were worth up to $2.6 billion. [545] However, a judge at the US International Trade Commission ruled that its image preview patent was invalid. [546]

The bonus issue was one of the most emotionally charged issues in bankruptcy court. It was opposed by the US Department of Justice, [547] and by many individual retirees. The president of an association of approximately five thousand retirees wrote a two-page letter to the judge

---

542 See note 521, supra.

543 See *The Value Line Investment Survey,* April 27, 2012, 1981.

544 *The Wall Street Journal,* "Fujifilm Thrived by Changing Focus," Jan. 20, 2012, B5.

545 See *The Wall Street Journal,* "Kodak's Patent Allure Fades," June 9 and 10, 2012, B1.

546 See *The Wall Street Journal,* "Kodak Patent Tossed by Judge," May 22, 2012, B5.

547 See *online.wsj.com,* "Justice Unit Fights Kodak Executive Bonus Plan," July 31, 2012.

arguing against payment of any bonuses.[548] In a poll of eight hundred readers of *Rochester Business Journal,* 89 percent thought payment of bonuses was a bad idea, and only 11 percent thought it was a good idea.[549]

Despite the unpopularity of payment of bonuses, the bankruptcy court sided with the company in a written order dated August 8, 2012.[550] Had the venue of the bankruptcy court been in Rochester, the judge would have been under peer pressure to rule otherwise. This could possibly explain why Kodak filed in the Southern District of New York rather than upstate in Kodak's hometown. There is no record of any formal objection by the retirees to the New York City venue of the bankruptcy. Since a great many retirees resided in the Rochester area, the venue would have been more appropriate for them in the Western District of New York. In any event, the payment of bonuses was inconsistent with the earlier reforms of George Fisher: 50 percent based on shareholder satisfaction, 30 percent based on market-share growth, and 20 percent based on increasing the employment of women and minorities.[551]

The bonus plan in the judge's order was known as "EXCEL." It had been effective since January 1, 2002.[552]

---

548 12-10202-alg, Document 1805.

549 *Rochester Business Journal,* July 20, 2012.

550 12-10202-alg, Document 1838.

551 Footnote 54, supra.

552 Notice of 2003 Annual Meeting and Proxy Statement dated Mar. 28, 2003, 111.

Aggrieved investors and retirees had a full and fair opportunity to previously challenge the EXCEL plan, but they had refrained from doing so for almost ten years. Because of Kodak's failure to meet its mid- 2007 objective of digital profitability,[553] Kodak had not excelled. Did Kodak excel by spending $301 million to repurchase its stock at $15.01 per share?[554] Did Kodak excel by losing its 2010 "momentum"?[555] Did Kodak excel by failing to profitably commercialize the digital camera, which it had invented in 1975?[556] Did Kodak excel by filing for bankruptcy? In what did Kodak actually excel?

As explained in its 2003 Proxy Statement, executive compensation had three components: (1) base salaries, (2) short-term variable pay, and (3) long-term incentives. The short-term variable pay was based on EXCEL (Executive Compensation for Excellence and Leadership). The two key metrics were (a) revenue growth and (b) economic profit.[557] As of December 31, 2002, Kodak's Executive Compensation and Development Committee (ECDC) had control of the company's executive compensation plans. The Committee consisted of four independent directors.[558]

---

553 Footnote 287, supra.

554 Footnote 395, supra.

555 Footnote 427, supra.

556 Footnote 533, supra.

557 Kodak Notice of Annual Meeting of Shareholders and Proxy Statement dated Mar. 28, 2003, 111.

558 Ibid, 110.

By December 31, 2003, the ECDC consisted of six independent directors.[559] While revenue growth remained one of the two metrics in the EXCEL plan, investable cash flow replaced economic profit as the other metric.[560]

Kodak's Notice of 2011 Annual Meeting and Proxy Statement was its last prior to its bankruptcy filing. By March 16, 2011, the ECDC had grown to eight independent directors.[561] The metric had substantially changed. Gone were any metrics for revenue growth or investable cash flow. Instead, the new metrics were (1) cash generation before restructuring payments and (2) digital revenue growth, and (3) total segment earnings from operations.[562]

Intellectual property revenues had previously been reported   as sales by the company.[563] This again raised the issue of how to measure revenue. Also at issue was the scope of discretion in the board's compensation committee to alter metrics of the EXCEL plan to compensate executives while the company's finances deteriorated.

While the bankruptcy court awaited the results of Kodak's patent auction, the company issued a press release that it would sell other businesses. Included in the sale were 105,000 picture kiosks, and the company's

---

559 Kodak Notice of 2004 Annual Meeting and Proxy Statement dated April 6, 2004, 117.

560 Ibid, 119.

561 Kodak Notice of 2011 Annual Meeting and Proxy Statement dated Mar. 31, 2011, 35.

562 Ibid, 36.

563 Footnote 434, supra.

photographic paper and film business.[564] Thus, in a period of approximately six months, Kodak decided to stop selling cameras and film, a business it had taken more than a century to build.

Doubts began to arise over the viability of Kodak's strategy to exit bankruptcy. It was reported that initial bids at the patent auction were only ten percent of Kodak's valuation of its patent portfolio.[565] In its press release announcing the sale of its film business, Kodak hinted that it might "retain" its patent portfolio.[566] Also, a competitor announced that it would "wind down" its inkjet printing business.[567] Although this action could benefit Kodak by removing a competitor, it was also evidence of the weakness of the market for inkjet printers.

As Kodak's cash burn increased from $43 million in May to $64 million in June to $72 million in July, Kodak responded with its usual remedy: more layoffs.[568] In addition to the previous 2,700 layoffs in 2012, Kodak announced an additional 1000 layoffs before the year's end. Included were its chief financial officer and chief operating officer, Philip Faraci.[569]

---

564 Press Release, Aug. 23, 2012.

565 "Kodak to Sell Film Business That Made It a Blue Chip." *The Wall Street Journal*, Aug. 24, 2012.

566 Footnote 564, supra.

567 "Lexmark to Wind Down Inkjet-Printing Business," *The Wall Street Journal*, Aug. 29, 2012.

568 "Kodak CFO Leaves; More Jobs Cut," *The Wall Street Journal*, Sept. 11, 2012, B7.

569 "Eastman Kodak to cut more jobs," *Reuters*, Sept. 10, 2012.

Mr. Faraci had been Kodak's president and chief operating officer since September 2007 and had spent twenty-two years at Hewlett-Packard, where he was senior vice president and general manager for the Inkjet Imaging Solutions Group.[570]

The results of the patent auction were originally scheduled to be announced on August 20, 2012. It was repeatedly adjourned:

1. To August 30, 2012.
2. To September 7, 2012.
3. To September 19, 2012.
4. "Until further notice."

In a notice filed in court on September 14, 2012, Kodak stated that it "may not reach acceptable terms with parties via the Auction Process," and indicated it might retain its patents, or create a "newly formed licensing company."[571]

It is now necessary to decide whether or not a continuing narrative of events in the bankruptcy court would add anything important. Whether or not Kodak would emerge from bankruptcy, one thing is clear: the company founded by George Eastman to popularize photography was no more. Tens of thousands of its loyal workers had been laid off, much of its real estate had been sold, many factories had been demolished, and it stopped making cameras and film. In the event it exited bankruptcy, it would be "Kodak" in name only. It was the victim of a

---

570 Eastman Kodak Company Form 10-K Annual Report for the year ended Dec. 31, 2010, 16.

571 12-10202-alg, Document 2019.

reverse Midas touch, in which its transformation into a digital photography company had failed. Should the company successfully exit bankruptcy, a more fitting name would be "Eastman Printing Company." The name "Kodak" was identified with cameras and film, but that business was dead.

Driving South on Lake Avenue past the demolished buildings in what was once Kodak Park towards Kodak's World Headquarters at 343 State Street brings to mind the famous poem by Percy Bysshe Shelley:

OZYMANDIAS

I met a traveler from an antique land,
Who said – "Two vast and trunkless legs of stone
Stand in the desert... Near them, on the sand,
Half sunk a shattered visage lies, whose frown,
And wrinkled lip, and sneer of cold command,
Tell that its sculptor well those passions read
Which yet survive, stamped on these lifeless things,
The hand that mocked them, and the heart that fed;
And on the pedestal, these words appear.
My name is Ozymandias, King of Kings,
Look on my Works, ye Mighty, and despair!
Nothing beside remains. Round the decay
Of that colossal Wreck, boundless and bare
The lone and level sands stretch far away."

Table of Contents - Point III
[*new*]
Analysis And Update

Point III

Analysis and Update

10 - KODAK WAS A WEAPON OF MASS JOB DESTRUCTION

Kodak emerged from Bankruptcy on September 3, 2013. According to its 2015 Annual Report Kodak employed 6,400 people at the end of 2015. Thirty (30) years before in 1985 Kodak had employed 128,950 people. Thus, Kodak lost 122,550 jobs in thirty (30) years. This amounts to an <u>average loss of 4,085 jobs per year</u>.

The deleterious effects which Kodak's downsizing had on the Rochester community were previously explored in the first pages of Chapter 8. According to an article in the March 22, 2015 *New York Times* Rochester's murder rate was five (5) times that of New York City, and the CEO lived on the West Coast. Who could blame him for that? It was not just snowy winters, chemical pollution, Main Street filled with vacant and boarded-up stores, low professional salaries, high health insurance costs, lack of free automobile parking, contaminated water, and high taxes that deterred people from living in Rochester. It was unsafe and dangerous to live there. If you lived there, you could be murdered.

11 – KODAK DISSIPATED MORE THAN $7 BILLION ON FAILED INVESTMENTS

Common Stock Purchases of EK shares –

2000 – Kodak bought 21.6 million shares at $41 per share - **$885,600,000.00**

Dec. 31, 2008 - Kodak bought 20 million shares at an average price of $15.01 per share - **$300,000,200.00**.

	$885,600,000.00
	$300,000,200.00
TOTAL	**$1,185,600,200.00**

Purchases of other companies-

1981- ATEX - $79.8 million.

2003- (1). Applied Science Fiction - $32 million.

(2). MiraMedica – undisclosed price.

(3). LaserPacific - $30.5 million.

(4). Practice Works - $486 million.

(5). Algotec Systems - $42.5 million.

(6). Scitex digital printing - $250 million.

1981 and 2003 – at least $920,800,000.00

Note: 2003 purchases were partially funded by the Sept. 23, 2003 reduction in the common stock dividend from $.90 per share to $.25 per share. Also, in 1993 Kodak had sold its digital printing company to Scitex for $70 million. Ten years later Kodak bought it back for more than triple the price it had sold it.

China   In 1998 Kodak decided to invest almost $1 billion in Chinese manufacturing plants. By the end of 2004 almost 95% of Kodak's cameras were made there. On May 2, 2007 Kodak announced a **$220 million** charge for closing the Chinese buildings.

SUMMARY	Purchases of EK common stock	$1,185,600,200.00
	Purchases of other companies	$ 920,800,000.00
	China writeoff	$ 220,000,000.00
	SUBTOTAL	**$2,326,400,200.00**
	Sterling Drug +	5,100,000,000.00
	TOTAL	**$7,426,400,200.00**

12 – KODAK FAILED TO PROFITABLY COMMERCIALIZE ITS SCIENTIFIC INVENTIONS

Kodak claimed to have invented the digital camera in the 1970's. Instead of then commercializing its digital camera, Kodak went off on a tangent.

First, it plagiarized Polaroid Land cameras at the cost of a patent infringement judgment in the sum of **$909,500,000.00.**

Second, it reduced the size of its film from 35mm [EK size 135], to Instamatic format [EK size 126], to Disc film. 35 mm film did not fit inside Instamatic cameras, and Instamatic film did not fit inside Disc cameras. Using the same film in progressively smaller format sizes was symptomatic of Kodak's failure of nerve. It was akin to reducing the size of a computer screen, attempting to obsolete prior hardware, forcing consumers to buy new cameras and film. The Disc camera negative was so small that regular size prints were excessively grainy and not sharp. The product was a failure.

Rather than market a breakthrough digital camera, Kodak tried to prolong traditional film photography with its Advanced Photo System (APS).

Kodak incorrectly praised APS as the "most significant consumer product introduction in 30 years."   It wasn't. That description exemplifies Kodak's self-delusion, and failure to confront the painful reality that its cash cow was soon to be obsolete.

13 – KODAK FAILED TO FORESEE THE SPEED WITH WHICH DIGITAL PHOTOGRAPHY WOULD REPLACE FILM

In 1990 Kodak forecast that in 2020 thirty per cent (30%) of all photos would be digital. Hence, it also forecast that in 2020 seventy per cent (70%) of all photos would be traditional film.

Thirteen (13) years later in 2003 Kodak President Carp stated that after 2006, "we'll see a <u>slow decay</u> [emphasis added] of film in the United States." Later in 2003 he stated, "...The consumer traditional business is going to begin <u>a slow decline</u> [emphasis added] though it's not going to fall off a cliff."

In 2004 film sales declined 18%, and in 2005 Kodak estimated film sales would decline 30%.

In 2005 Kodak decided to partially write off its film manufacturing operations in China.

Thus, Kodak forecasted a slow decline of film, but the decline was fast.

14 – UNDER FINANCIAL PRESSURE KODAK FAILED TO LINK EXECUTIVE COMPENSATION TO CORPORATE PERFORMANCE

In 1989 the Chairman's pay increased 20 percent and the President's pay increased 24%. This was in spite of the loss of the Polaroid lawsuit, layoffs, restructuring, and a decline in corporate earnings.

In 1995 George Fischer had attempted to reform Kodak's compensation by linking it to shareholder satisfaction, market-share growth, and increasing employment of women and minorities.

In 2009 Kodak suspended its dividend and discontinued Kodachrome. Standard and Poor's downgraded Kodak's debt to junk status. Its sales declined 19% and it had a net loss from continuing operations. It increased the compensation of its top two executives by $6,807,498.00. This conflicted with the Company's stated "key priorities for 2009:" "Align the Company's cost structure with external economic realities."

Hence, Kodak ignored the George Fischer reforms, and reverted to its earlier ways.

15 – KODAK SACRIFICED AMERICAN WORKERS IN FAVOR OF FOREIGN WORKERS

While it is difficult or impossible to discern management's intentions, facts are facts, and the facts do not lie. In 1995 Kodak employed 316 workers in China, and employed 54,400 workers in the USA. In 2000 Kodak employed 5556 workers in China, and 43,200 workers in the USA. In the five years from 1995 to 2000 Kodak lost 11,200 American workers or about 21% of its American workers. In that same period Kodak gained 5,240 Chinese workers; its Chinese workers increased 16 times.

In 1998 Kodak announced it planned to invest possibly $1 billion in several Chinese photography companies. Kodak would build its first new photographic film plant in 30 years.

In 2002 Kodak moved production of its one-time use cameras to China and Mexico.

By the end of 2004 almost 95% of Kodak's cameras were made in China, where workers were paid about $5.75 per day.

Even low Chinese labor costs could not offset the technological obsolescence of film. In 2007 it closed its Chinese film sensitizing operations, and took write-offs. It thus wasted almost $1 billion on a failed attempt to outsource manufacturing to cheap labor in foreign countries.

16 – KODAK AGAIN LOST MONEY AFTER BEING DISCHARGED FROM BANKRUPTCY

Kodak filed for Bankruptcy on Jan. 19, 2012. This was done after the then CEO had stated, "...There is no reason in the world to believe that we will be in that (position) in any scenario that we can imagine." It used Bankruptcy Court to attempt avoid paying almost $48 million to several retailers. It emerged with an allegedly clean slate on Sept. 3, 2013.

By 2015 Kodak was again in the red. In 2015 it had a net loss of $75 million. If terminating more than 100,000 employees and going Bankrupt could not make Kodak profitable, then what could? To Kodak the glass was half full. In its press release disclosing the $75 million loss it emphasized that it had exceeded its earnings goal for the year.

In the press release the CEO spoke of delivering "strong operating performance..." If losing $75 million is strong operating performance, then what is weak operating performance? Would Kodak ever have a profitable year in the future? If so, when would this happen?

Kodak ignored GAAP measures in its 2016 guidance in favor of "Operational EBITDA." Since it had "Operational EBITDA of $122 million in 2015 (although it had a GAAP loss of $75 million), and it projected "Operational EBITDA" of $130 million to $150 million in 2016, this, in Kodak's opinion, was great progress. But by GAAP standards, would it still lose money in 2016? When, if ever, would it have a profit by GAAP standards? GAAP means Generally Accepted Accounting Principles. "Operational EBITDA" was little more than an Orwellian Newspeak type of euphemism for losing money without explicitly saying so.

In view of Kodak's inability to operate with a profit, one wonders if instead of trying to rehabilitate the troubled company, the Bankruptcy Court should have ordered its dissolution, equitably distributing the remaining assets to the creditors and shareholders and former employees.

Who would or should invest in Kodak stock based upon "Operational EBITDA?" Why buy stock of a company that can't earn a profit?

17 – WHAT SHOULD KODAK HAVE DONE DIFFERENTLY?

According to the April 22, 2016 issue of *The Value Line Investment Survey* in 2015 Fujifilm had more than $21 billion in annual sales, employed more than 78,000 people, and paid a 1.6% dividend. Its market capitalization was only 13% debt.

Ironically, one of Fuji's best-selling products was its Instax picture-in-a minute film camera. While it continued to make digital cameras, it had also successfully diversified into healthcare, including management of hospital data. It even continued to make traditional film.

In Chapter 25 of *The Prince* Machiavelli cautioned about the man who remains constant as times change. Kodak failed to change with the times. It was inflexible in its dogmatic adherence to traditional film, when the world preferred digital imaging. "At Kodak we don't worry about the market. We *are* the market." Famous last words.

What should Kodak have done differently?

(1) Instead of buying a third-rate pharmaceutical company like Sterling Drug, it should have bought research leaders Pfizer or Merck.

(2) It should have retained the Eastman Chemical Company, and not spun it off to shareholders.

(3) It should have continued to produce Kodachrome film, which had fade-resistant archival properties, which could have been marketed to consumers and institutions as something that could survive the wear and tear of aging; something that made almost permanent images.

(4) It should have merged with Adobe Systems, in order to obtain a foothold in imaging software.

(5) It should hired management from Adobe Systems to run the entire Eastman Kodak Company.

(6) It should have moved corporate headquarters from Rochester, NY to Silicon Valley.

(7) It should not have invested in China.

(8) It should not have made clones of the Polaroid Land Camera.

(9) It should have linked executive compensation to corporate GAAP earnings, and the common stock price.

(10) Most important, it should have stayed in closer contact with consumers. It should not have tried to persuade consumers to buy old technology which they did not want.

CONCLUSION

KODAK FAILED TO SUCCESSFULLY ADAPT TO THE RAPID RATE OF CHANGE IN THE ADOPTION OF DIGITAL FILMLESS PHOTOGRAPHY

The End

INDEX

A

B

P

R

S

T

U

V

W

X

Appendix: A Note on Sources

As a former shareholder of Eastman Kodak stock, the author maintained a file of news clippings about the company. For more than thirty years, whenever a story about Kodak was printed in a newspaper or business magazine, he clipped it and threw it into a file. This file became the source material for this book. Among the many sources were the following:

Associated Press

Barron's – published by Dow Jones

Bloomberg.com

Business Week – published by McGraw-Hill (before acquisition by Bloomberg)

EF Hutton (investment summaries)

Forbes, published by Forbes, LLC.

Fortune, published by Time, Inc.

McKeown's Price Guide to Antique Classic Cameras, 12th Edition, 2005–2006

Reuters

Syracuse.com

The Financial Times

The Kodak Park Works—Where Kodak Films, Papers, and Chemicals Are Made, Eastman Kodak Company, 1964

The New York Times

Rochester Business Journal

Rochester Democrat and Chronicle, by Gannett Rochester Newspapers

TheStreet.com

The Value Line Investment Survey, published by Value Line Publishing, LLC

The Wall Street Journal – published by Dow Jones

YAHOO! News, and YAHOO! Finance

Company-specific documents were obtained from the website SEC.gov and from documents posted on-line in Kodak's bankruptcy proceeding. These documents include the following:

Miscellaneous Kodak Press Releases.

Eastman Kodak Company Annual Report Forms 10-K for the years ending December 31, 1999–December 31, 2010.

Eastman Kodak Company Annual Report Form 10-K/A for the year ending Dec. 31, 2011.

"Kodak Transforms" official company website re: Chap. XI Reorganization.

Numerous Company Notices of Annual Meeting and Proxy Statements.

United States Bankruptcy Court – Southern District of New York, Case No. 12-10202 (ALG).

Printed in Great Britain
by Amazon